To : Judith

♡, Dana

~ Aug. 2018 ~

Enjoy ! ☺

Praise for *Hunting Hope*

You hold in your hands something more than a book. This is a candle. Use it to find your way in the dark. This heartfelt book, written by a gifted storyteller, will awaken hope and inspire bravery in its readers—no matter what season they're in.

Jennifer Dukes Lee, Author of *Love Idol*

Pain and suffering are considered as vehicles for grace in Maples's bold exploration of how she overcame struggles to find solace in Scripture and the presence of God. Readers will appreciate Maples's candor as she lays out her pain and feelings of inadequacy in plain sight, and will find comfort in her uplifting lessons for overcoming personal difficulties of any kind.

Publishers Weekly

Pain and suffering are found in unexpected places along life's journey. They often surprise us and leave us trying to find where to take our next step. As followers of the way of Jesus, we must prepare in the light for what we will do when darkness comes. Nika's work in *Hunting Hope* will be a lantern of strong light for those searching for a glimpse of Him, of His presence. I highly recommend this book for those in darkness now but also for those wanting to prepare for either their own journeys or to help another through the journey of uncertainty.

Beverly Ross, MA, LPC,
Founder and Executive Director,
Wise County Christian Counseling

In *Hunting Hope*, Nika provides a guidebook of sorts for the sufferer, illuminating the path toward clarity and meaning, even when the suffering itself seems to have no meaning at all. Through her own heartbreaking—or rather, heart-enriching—journey, Nika uses wit, wisdom, and humor to reveal the hidden treasures offered by God Himself through suffering . . . if only we have eyes and courage to see it.

Jason McArthur, Vice President of Artists & Repertoire,
Record Label Executive,
Provident Label Group/Sony Music Entertainment

Nika knows firsthand that hope begins with hurt, and that it is precisely for those hopeless moments that we need to be a hopeful person. But Nika knows that kind of hope doesn't come naturally to anyone, you have to hunt for it, her's is a voice I'd highly commend for your quest.

Jonathan Storment, Preaching Minister,
Highland Church of Christ, Abilene, Texas,
Author of *How To Start a Riot*, and
Co-author of *Bringing Heaven to Earth*

Nika brilliantly reminds us that pain and trials can, indeed, be gifts from God. This book is amazing for those in the midst of suffering, but possibly even better for the preparation of suffering that inevitably will come. Nika's transparency and storytelling ability fiercely point me toward the great Comforter and Healer.

Rob Thomas, CEO and President of RT Creative Group,
Parent Company of Graceway & Igniter Media

HUNTING HOPE

DIG THROUGH *the* DARKNESS *to* FIND *the* LIGHT

NIKA MAPLES

WORTHY®
Inspired

Published by Worthy Inspired, an imprint of Worthy Publishing Group, a division of Worthy Media, Inc.,
One Franklin Park, 6100 Tower Circle, Suite 210, Franklin, TN 37067.
WORTHY is a registered trademark of Worthy Media, Inc.

HELPING PEOPLE EXPERIENCE THE HEART OF GOD

Library of Congress Cataloging-in-Publication Data

Names: Maples, Nika.
Title: Hunting hope : dig through the darkness to find the light / by Nika
  Maples.
Description: Franklin, TN : Worthy Publishing, 2016. | Includes
  bibliographical references.
Identifiers: LCCN 2015042217 | ISBN 9781617956652 (hardcover)
Subjects: LCSH: Hope--Religious aspects--Christianity. | Suffering--Religious
  aspects--Christianity.
Classification: LCC BV4638 .M36 2016 | DDC 248.8/6--dc23
LC record available at http://lccn.loc.gov/2015042217

ISBN: 978-1-61795-665-2

For foreign and subsidiary rights, contact rights@worthypublishing.com

Cover Design: Connie Gabbert

Printed in the United States of America
16 17 18 19 20 21 LBM 10 9 8 7 6 5 4 3 2 1

CONTENTS

PART TWO: Our Character

To Candy

We were hunting for hope,

but what we found was a miracle.

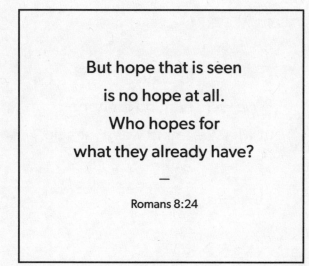

But hope that is seen
is no hope at all.
Who hopes for
what they already have?

—

Romans 8:24

THE DARK SEASON

The day is Yours, the night also is Yours;
You have prepared the light and the sun.
You have set all the borders of the earth;
You have made summer and winter.

Psalm 74:16–17 NKJV

OUR HEARTS ARE SHIVERING. We're asking, "How long will this last?"

Life used to be lovely, but then the wind changed. The temperature dropped, and it hasn't risen in weeks. Now night falls sooner than it did, and the morning is always gray. Pleasure and joy are tattered leaves. Our golden October is gone. We have walked into winter. The dark season has come. When it happens, we cannot see the end of it. On this and every day there is a frozen forecast:

Disappointment. Disillusionment. Depression. Despair.

All we can think about is the way it used to be. We're afraid that if we're out in the cold long enough, we'll forget how it feels to be warm, to be happy. We'll start to believe that winter will last forever.

The next question burns like frostbite on our lips: "Where is God?"

Here is the truth: God is in the dark season with us. He makes "darkness his covering, his canopy around him—the dark rain clouds of the sky."[1] God is enthroned in mystery and is comfortable in the clouded unknown. Only His offspring are not. Where the path grows dim, we steer away. When pain casts a shadow, we shrink back. Most people run *toward* ease and *from* difficulty. Few will leave comfort in order to climb to the secret places.

Moses did. In Exodus we read, "The people remained at a distance, while Moses approached the thick darkness where God was."[2] He was willing to scale a dark mountain in order to get to God.

Moses was a hope hunter.

Hope is not an accident. Hunting it takes courage. Hope hunters seem to command a storehouse of resilience during hard times; they make it look so easy to stay positive that we tend to overlook the dirt beneath their fingernails and the sweat on their shirts. We forget that people who have hope have worked to take hold of it. Hope hunters know how to excavate. They rake through the rubble of an unwanted situation to bring forth what is buried beneath. Dark days don't slow down their digging.

They dig into difficult circumstances because they have come to expect that adversity will produce good.

Moses knew there was more in the dark, and he didn't want to miss a bit of it. The desperation he felt in the wilderness motivated him to think like a hunter, to search out every trace of the Creator's hand, to listen for His whispered voice. Moses chased and climbed and called and cried out for something greater. Difficulty didn't put him off; it spurred him on. And Moses was not the only one.

Paul was a hope hunter too.

The esteemed apostle describes the phenomenon of hope hidden in hardship by describing his own dark season:

In everything we do, we show that we are true ministers of God. We patiently endure troubles and hardships and calamities of every kind. We have been beaten, been put in prison, faced angry mobs, worked to exhaustion, endured sleepless nights, and gone without food. We prove ourselves by our purity, our understanding, our patience, our kindness, by the Holy Spirit within us, and by our sincere love. We faithfully preach the truth. God's power is working in us. We use the weapons of righteousness in the right hand for attack and the left hand for defense. We serve God whether people honor us or despise us, whether they slander us or praise us. We are honest, but they call us impostors. We are ignored, even though we are well known. We live close to death, but we are still alive. We have been beaten, but we have not been killed. Our hearts ache, but we always have joy. We are poor, but we give spiritual riches to others. We own nothing, and yet we have everything.[3]

The gleam of confidence in this passage blinds me. Shock comes when I try to focus on the sentence Paul writes just before he pens this horrifying list of trouble. We can see his shining faith as he declares, "I tell you, now is the time of God's favor, now is the day of salvation."[4]

What?!

Now, Paul? Now is the time of God's *favor*?! When you are whipped and starved? Now is the day of *salvation*?! When you are imprisoned and mistreated? When you are "worked to exhaustion"? When you are slandered, ignored, and poor?

I cannot make sense of it. But Paul wholeheartedly believes that God is working good into and through his difficulty. He expects to see God in the dark so he looks for Him with a hunter's eyes, narrowed and ready.

There are plenty of places in Scripture where the Lord clearly separates Himself from darkness. Again and again, we read truths like this: "God is light; in him there is no darkness at all."[5] And, "The light shines in the darkness, and the darkness can never extinguish it."[6] Even Jesus comforts His disciples by saying, "I am the light of the world. If you follow me, you won't have to walk in darkness, because you will have the light that leads to life."[7]

Yet to read a Scripture that assures "there is no darkness at all" in God and then misconstrue that God has nothing to do with darkness robs us of precious understanding. The Bible explains that there is no *spiritual darkness* in God. There is no wickedness, no sin, no evil, no spot or blemish. There is no defect. He is the only Purity there ever has been. But none of these verses suggests that God has nothing to do with *situational darkness*.

We must always flee from spiritual darkness and evil, but we do not have to fight and kick and wrestle and run from situational darkness, which usually comes in the form of a circumstance we don't want. Some situations are very dark, indeed. But not every painful event in life is due to an evil attack. Some are a part of living in the natural world.

Others are brought about by the Lord. All of them can be used by God for good. The prophet Isaiah records these words from the mouth of Jehovah: "I form the light and create darkness, I make peace and create calamity; I, the LORD, do all these things."[8]

God is not afraid of the dark. Darkness is part of His design for the universe. He thought of it, making space for it throughout the earth. God carved ocean depths with just a word. He shadowed the deep forest places. He emptied caverns. He summoned nightfall. He crafted the kangaroo's cradling pouch.

He thought of winter.

Look through any January window to see a stunning truth in naked branches. Winter is not a fluke. Winter is every bit as God-ordained, as blessed and necessary, as are the other three seasons. We've seen the annual repetition long enough to be sure that spring is coming, even when we cannot see the evidence. We believe that barren trees will again give birth, and our faith in this succession never falters. No matter how disheartening the day, we know new life is on the way. We trust the natural seasons so even in a long and bitter winter, we hold on and wait for the weather to change. The hope of spring sustains us.

When it comes to the spiritual seasons, though, our trust weakens, especially during a dark season of difficulty.

For all the frost we feel, we cannot sense a coming spring, so we waste time wondering where the cold came from and why.

Trying to find the reason for our winters is like trying to see the wind. Maybe the *source* of a dark season isn't as important as the *result* of a dark season. Maybe it doesn't matter what *causes suffering* in our lives nearly as much as it matters what *suffering causes* in our lives. If adversity brings about bitterness, fury, and disbelief in the Lord, then it will be a loss. But if it brings about humility, patience, and dependence upon the Lord, then it will be for His glory.

Questions about suffering are questions about sovereignty. Either God is in control, or He isn't. If God is in control, then what we know about *God* is more important than what we know about *our circumstances*.

God is always in control. This assurance becomes the hope hunters' compass. It's what sets them on their quest. They know He can sweep away the ashes, or He can fashion our ashes into beauty. They know He can strip our coats of heaviness, or He can transform them into garments of praise.[9] The hope hunter's response to obstacles is always to surrender to God's work through our trials. God is *for* us, not against us.[10] Perhaps our best question is not "How could You let this happen *to* me, Lord?" but "How are You using this *for* me, Lord?"

Part of the way the Lord uses challenges *for* us is our character formation. Many significant individuals in the Bible experienced a period of time when they were positioned in a dark and unexpected place in preparation for a divine assignment. We see the chilling precedent in Scripture: Darkness was an initiation. Darkness preceded new life and new work. Darkness was the beginning of things.

- In the darkness of a dungeon, Joseph received his commission and became a government official.
- In the darkness of midnight, Gideon realized his identity and became an invincible warrior.
- In the darkness of a fish's belly, Jonah reconciled with God and became a missionary.
- In the darkness of insomnia, Samuel recorded God's voice and became a prophet.
- In the darkness of a lions' den, Daniel recognized God as the King of the beasts and became an evangelist to royalty.
- In the darkness of the tomb, Lazarus was resurrected and became an example of new life in Jesus.
- In the darkness of blind eyes, Paul resolved to live for Christ and became a father of the Church.

- And through the darkness of death, Jesus rose to rescue humanity and reign as the Savior of the world.

Darkness became part of the plan. These men not only accepted their dark, they learned to *see* in the dark. And what they saw was God.

God is earth's only hope, so He wants leaders who will never lose sight of Him. That's why when God needs a leader, He makes a hope hunter. The hard truth is: hope hunters are made in the dark.

There can be important training in our trials. Joseph speaks of this fact. He has every right to retaliate against his spiteful, spineless brothers, but he tells them, "You intended to harm me, but God intended it for good to accomplish what is now being done, the saving of many lives."[11]

Clearly, Joseph was a hope hunter. A man without hope cannot call a trial a blessing.

When an outcome so miraculous comes from an experience so difficult, we have to admit that we do not know how to define what is good. A blessing isn't what makes us comfortable or happy. A blessing is what brings us closer to the Lord and to the center of His will. In the end, the center of His will is the only thing that will satisfy us. I have never met a person who wanted to go through a season of difficulty. But I also have never met a sincere believer who didn't want to be close to God and to experience His great works on their behalf. We may not desire to go through trials, however, the Bible tells us that through surrendering our suffering, we share in Christ's death so that we may know the power of His resurrection in us.[12]

If this is true, then when a trial comes our way, will we say no?

As crazy as it sounds, when tragedy came into the lives of the apostles, they didn't say no; they *rejoiced*. Joy is the mark of a master hope hunter:

> *In all this you greatly rejoice, though now for a little while you may have had to suffer grief in all kinds of trials. These have come so that the proven genu- ineness of your faith—of greater worth than gold, which perishes even though refined by fire—may result in praise, glory and honor when Jesus Christ is revealed.*[13]

I can hardly do this. But I believe the Bible, and it says that we too can rejoice if we do not allow ourselves to give way to fear.[14] The *only* way we can live without fear is to put our trust in the One who holds the world, our hearts, and every season in His loving hands.

Because we know God *can* end our dark seasons instantly, we know there is a reason when He *doesn't*. He might be preparing us for new life and new work. This could be our initiation. The hunger is where our hearts learn to hunt.

Fear will try to find us while we're here. We will never have to go looking for doubt or anxiety. They will strut straight into our camp. But hope will be hidden. Hope remains camouflaged in the daily mundane, and if we aren't looking for it, we will miss it even though it is right before our eyes. Hope is something we must pursue. Until we apprehend it, we have to be rugged men and women who *know* and *do* specific things in order to survive in the wild.

Know. Then do. Because darkness always gives way to light.

WHAT DO WE KNOW?

Hope hunters secure themselves with biblical truths about God's character. How we see God will affect how we see our circumstances. But if we are not careful, how we see our circumstances will affect how we see God. This cannot be! Hope hunters are proactive. They come back to the Bible to calibrate their minds. The best way to know who God is by reading who He says He is in His Word.

WHAT DO WE DO?

Hope hunters take action based on biblical truth. After our knowledge of God's character has been established, we allow Him to work on our character. What we do in the dark season makes a difference. We should only do what He says to do in His Word.

His Word is what we need to *know* and what we need to *do*. Psalm 147:18 confirms the power of Scripture: "He sends his word, and it melts [the icy blast]." We may be traveling in the arctic territory of our hearts, but God has sent His Word to warm the way before us. He melts through the places where we would slip and paves our paths with promises.

Hope is on the advance, and we can't just stay where we are and expect to take hold of it. We must scan the bleak horizon, set our eyes without the slightest turning, and chase it through the ice.

Every season is open season on hope.

PART ONE
GOD'S CHARACTER

Those who are wise will take all this to heart;
they will see in our history
the faithful love of the LORD.

Psalm 107:43 NLT

CHAPTER ONE

HE LET IT HAPPEN

---

*God, who made the world and everything in it, since He is
Lord of heaven and earth, does not dwell in temples made
with hands. Nor is He worshiped with men's hands,
as though He needed anything, since He gives to all life,
breath, and all things. And He has made from one blood
every nation of men to dwell on all the face of the earth, and
has determined their preappointed times and the boundaries
of their dwellings, so that they should seek the Lord,
in the hope that they might grope for Him and find Him,
though He is not far from each one of us;
for in Him we live and move and have our being.*

Acts 17:24–28 NKJV

A FRIEND OF MINE owns sixteen heavily wooded acres
in east Texas. His wife has made their two-story log cabin,
complete with wraparound porch, so warm and charming,
it is worthy of a feature in *Southern Living* magazine. Every
crisply curtained window, every pitcher of wildflowers is

placed with mindful grace. Hummingbirds thrum in the eaves. Porch rockers creak with contentment. Around the cabin, my friend has kept the land and foliage with a similar elegance of attention for two decades.

A few years ago, he needed to clear a key area on their property so he took his tractor and chainsaw to fell some dying trees. It was something he had done many times. On the last tree of the day, he cut a large V-notch in the front of the trunk and headed back to the tractor to pull the chain around the tree. Before he started the engine, he heard an echoing pop behind him. The oak wasn't supposed to be coming down yet. He only remembers jumping off the tractor. It may have been close to an hour before he regained consciousness.

Facedown.

The oak lay beside him. Both of his forearms were in pieces. His collarbone had snapped. His T12 vertebra was broken. For another hour, he drew enough aching breath to yell for help. He had to. His cell phone had landed twenty feet away, on the other side of the tree.

Thank God for the warmth of Texas Februarys. A teenaged neighbor felt uncomfortably hot while playing video games and opened the windows to let in some air. He thought he heard a small voice calling, so he stopped, leaned and listened outside the window, but then went back to his chair and resumed the game. After stopping, going to the window, and restarting the game several times, he was convinced he must be hearing things.

Then he recognized the voice.

"It's Dr. Howard!" he yelled as he ran out the door, tearing through the woods to find his neighbor. Within minutes, an ambulance was on its way.

The paramedics placed Dr. Howard's twisted and injured body onto a gurney and sped to the hospital. Throughout the bumpy trip, my friend grimaced in pain until he saw an EMT brandishing large shears. Carefully, she lifted the leg of his overalls.

"No! Not the boots!" he yelled. "Cut off my clothes, but don't cut my boots!"

She paused, looked at him for a moment, then returned to her work.

A true Texan to the end, he hollered, "I said, 'not the boots!' Please! Those are brand-new boots, and I want to keep them! Just pull 'em off! I can take it! I can take it!"

"No," she answered coolly, and with a snip-snip, they were useless. His head fell back to the pillow in anguish. Losing his boots was the final blow.

But the EMT knew something about the present reality that my friend did not yet know. His foot had been crushed. He could *not* have endured the pain of pulling off his boots, as he'd thought he could. It was pointless to save them for the future anyway. After surgery, he would never be able to fit that foot into a standard pair of boots again.

• • •

It is easy to picture Dr. Howard's life-changing experience as he lay there in the woods, blinded by fireworks of pain. But it is difficult to picture God letting the big oak fall when He could have flicked it away like a matchstick. My friend never saw it coming, but we know that God did. Most of the time we don't see the crushing pain that will knock us flat either. But if we do happen to see terror on its way, the first thing we do is beg God to stay it with His hand. Jesus did this in the Garden of Gethsemane when He "*fell with his face to the ground* and prayed, 'My Father, if it is possible, may this cup be taken from me. Yet not as I will, but as you will.'"[1]

He fell *facedown*.

The loving Father heard this cry for help and let darkness fall anyway. How it must have hurt God's heart not to intervene. He allowed that fatal day to dawn, but it wasn't because He had stopped loving His Son. No, He loved Him fiercely all the while. And when God permits the worst of life to fall on our backs, it doesn't mean He has stopped loving us either. An outside observer may ask, "After all that, you still love Him?" Our lives can answer resolutely, "Yes, I still love Him, and He still loves *me*." He does not allow us to experience pain because He wants us to hurt. He allows pain because He knows we can grow and learn from all our experiences, even the painful ones. And that growth often brings us closer to Him because He walks with us through the pain.

In our darkest seasons, God is not hiding. He wants to be found. It is a truth that sends *me* facedown. Though we endure hardship until our backs are broken and our arms are in pieces, may we ever grope for Him until we find Him, for when we find Him, we find the unexpected blessing of suffering. Suffering is an unexpected blessing because it refines our character and makes us one with Christ. It can help us see something we would find no other way. We discover hope.

Hope starts with hardship. When we don't feel hardship, we don't even need hope. In the book of Romans, Paul urges us to "boast in the hope of the glory of God. Not only so, but we also glory in our sufferings, because we know that suffering produces perseverance; perseverance, character; and character, hope. And hope does not put us to shame, because God's love has been poured out into our hearts through the Holy Spirit, who has been given to us."[2]

According to this unusual maze, suffering starts the

winding way to hope, and its path passes through character. Not to put too fine a point on it, but suffering alone may not lead to character growth and hope in the unsaved life or in the life of a rebellious believer who refuses to cooperate with spiritual formation. And when Paul explains his view of adversity, he is not elevating suffering for suffering's sake. He does not suggest that suffering adds to salvation. No, he is assuring us that it is *nearness to God* that produces character and hope. It just happens to be that difficulty provides the best opportunity for nearness because when we have nothing left to lean on, we learn to lean on God.

According to Hebrews 11, sometimes referred to as "The Hall of Faith," we read that difficulty displays our faith to the watching world. There are too many accounts of adversity in the Hall of Faith to dismiss the idea. We tend to admire the people on this list, thinking they already *had* great faith. We often overlook the fact that their faith was perfected by the difficult things they did. Great faith did not enable them to meet a great challenge as much as great faith was the *result* of meeting a great challenge.

"*Against all hope*, Abraham in hope believed and so became the father of many nations," Romans 4:18–22 reads, explaining that he didn't try to avoid or deny the reality of his infertility. No, "he faced the fact that his body was as good as dead," but what he knew of God reinterpreted what he saw in his life, and he "was strengthened in his faith" as he continued to believe that God could do what He said He would do. The perfection of Abraham's faith was a process.

Peter explains that the tests of our faith perfect our faith:

> *These trials will show that your faith is genuine. It is being tested as fire tests and purifies gold—though your faith is far more precious than mere gold. So when your faith remains strong through many trials, it will bring you much praise and glory and honor on the day when Jesus Christ is revealed to the whole world.*[3]

In nature, winter kills off almost everything so that new life can grow. Pain is clarifying in a similar way. Suddenly the superficial things that seemed to matter so much are put into perspective, allowing us to refocus our priorities. While our feet are on this earthen floor, we will not understand all of the reasons why God does what He does. But just as the EMT cut off Dr. Howard's boots because she saw that the wound was far worse than he knew, sometimes God cuts things out of our lives to save us from deeper pain. He always has information that we do not—both the reality of the present and the fullness of the future.

Our task, then, is to make our lives a theocracy, letting

God rule. We have a great example to follow in that area. The life of Jesus indirectly connects Romans 8:28 and John 8:28. The passage in Romans tells us that "God causes everything to work together for the good of those who love God and are called according to his purpose for them" (NLT). Clearly, the goodness of God's plan is something Jesus knows. In the John passage, we see His knowledge inform His actions. He says, "I do nothing on my own but say only what the Father taught me" (NLT). Every day of His life, Jesus put aside His own will so that the Father's could be done through Him.

He knew that even if it hurt, everything would work together for good.

Suffering *refines* our character, and when we grow closer to God because of it, suffering *reveals* God's character. The Bible tells us that *faithfulness* is His character, and we see that clearly through the way He sustains us in our trials.[4] Jesus points to this idea when asked about the origin of suffering. By giving two strange answers, He suggests that there is something more to our trials than we have considered. The first answer occurs when He meets a blind man, and His disciples ask whether the blindness is due to sin.

"'It was not because of his sins or his parents' sins,' Jesus answered. 'This happened so the power of God could be seen in him.'"[5] Within moments, Jesus heals the blind man and restores his sight.

Later, one of Jesus' best friends becomes so ill he comes very close to death. Everyone mourns and worries until Jesus declares, "Lazarus's sickness will not end in death. No, it happened for the glory of God so that the Son of God will receive glory from this."[6] Of course, Lazarus *does* die, but then Jesus raises him to life again.

Both of these passages illustrate that when illness or death (or hardship of any kind) comes, the power and glory of God can shine through healing, even though that is not the *only* way. With or without healing, God's glory is resplendent through our trust in Him. The whole world pays attention when we cry out for an end to darkness, while at the same time believing that Christ is the only Light we need. Our dependence upon Him declares that He is enough, that His grace is sufficient for us.[7] We should always ask for a miracle, but while we wait, God's calming presence in our lives is a miracle in itself.

Yes, when we are healed, our lives point to the Great Physician.

But when we are grieving, our lives point to the Comforter.

When we are confused and anxious, our lives point to the Counselor.

When we are in need, our lives point to the Provider.

When we are alone, our lives point to the Lover.

When we are abandoned, our lives point to the Father.

Suffering isn't pointless.

It can always point to God.

CHAPTER TWO

HE KNOWS HOW MUCH IT HURTS

Keep your eyes on Jesus, who both began and finished this race we're in. Study how he did it. Because he never lost sight of where he was headed—that exhilarating finish in and with God—he could put up with anything along the way: Cross, shame, whatever. And now he's there, in the place of honor, right alongside God. When you find yourselves flagging in your faith, go over that story again, item by item, that long litany of hostility he plowed through.

Hebrews 12:2–3 MSG

MY NIECE HAD a mean-looking splinter in the palm of her hand, and she asked me for help. Part of the splinter was not too deep, and I thought I could pull it out quickly. But every time I came near her with tweezers she'd scream and jerk away. Her tears were enormous, and they plopped on my arms as I held her. She was scared to let me touch her so she pulled away from the idea of more pain. No amount of my smooth talk got the tweezers any closer. Finally, I distracted her and whisked the splinter out, but not without more tears. It felt like a trick to her.

I let her cry in my arms; I didn't throw her on the ground and walk away.

I didn't tell her to dry it up.

I didn't warn her that she'll know greater pain than a splinter when she grows up.

I did not tell her to get over it.

I knew how much it hurt her, even though it was a pain that was very small to me. I can remove a splinter from my own hand without the slightest concern. But I based my level of compassion on her level of discomfort with a splinter, not on mine. So I just held her, rocking her back and forth. I covered that place on her palm with a Band-Aid. I spoke to her tenderly. Even when she was down to soft sniffles, she stayed in my embrace a long time. It took her awhile to feel like getting up to go on with the day. In that moment, I could not make my niece believe that the sting of the tweezers was actually my kindness to her, so I just acted quickly and bandaged her wound. All of my actions were performed out of love, both the pain and the comfort, though my niece only understood the comfort.

In the same way, all of God's actions are performed out of love, even when we do not understand them. He does not tell us to get over our pain. He knows how much it hurts. When James 4:8 says, "Come near to God and he will come near to you," the image is one of comfort, not effort. God doesn't come near to us as a reward. We do not earn His presence by coming near to Him first. The truth is much simpler.

A father can easily wrap his arms around the child who comes to sit in his lap.

When I am brokenhearted, if I draw near to God, He speaks tenderly. Most often He does so through His written Word. The Bible is His voice. His voice! Nothing heals like the sound of it. It can be so soft and gentle that a space of stillness is required in order to hear Him. If we will be still, we will know He is God.[1] We will *know*. I need this awareness more than anything, so I consistently set aside a time of stillness to give Him the opportunity to wrap His arms around me. He comforts me, and I am greatly helped. Like my niece after her splinter, sometimes I need to be healed and held awhile before I am ready to go on with the day.

There is a picture of this in Hosea 6:1, as the prophet urges us to move toward our healing. "Come, let us return to the LORD," he writes. "He has torn us to pieces but he will heal us; he has injured us but he will bind up our wounds."

The Lord has "torn us to pieces" and "injured us"? Well,

He certainly is willing to wreck our expectations if it means pulling us off a path that leads away from His best for us. It is far better that our temporal lives be upended so that our eternal lives are not. Every act of God is for our good and issues out of love. Even the ones that hurt. Even when He whisks away things we wanted. God will take us into His arms and heal us when we turn our faces to Him as a response to pain.

I turn my face to Him with a Bible on my lap as I sit in an old clawfoot chair in the corner of my bedroom. I bought it at a thrift store and had it reupholstered so long ago that the bold floral fabric has had time to go out of style and come back in. A coffee ring stains the arm, and I have covered a rip with a flannel throw. The space could not be more modest or more special to me. As I sit in this very unholy chair, something holy happens every day. Here my spiritual eyes adjust to the dark, and I can see hope.

And hope is such a comfort.

Later, when I go on with my day, I bring that comforting hope with me, sharing it with others.

All praise to God, the Father of our Lord Jesus Christ. God is our merciful Father and the source of all comfort. He comforts us in all our troubles so that we can comfort others. When they are troubled, we will be able to give them the same comfort God has given us. For the more we suffer for Christ, the more God will shower us with his comfort through Christ. Even when we are weighed down with troubles, it is for your comfort and salvation! For when we ourselves are comforted, we will certainly comfort you. Then you can patiently endure the same things we suffer. We are confident that as you share in our sufferings, you will also share in the comfort God gives us.[2]

The person with a naturally resilient heart often faces trouble and thinks, *I can do this. I don't need any help. I am fine. Fine.* There are a lot of times I have caught myself thinking this way. Some might say that it is a risky mind-set to have, one based in denial. Denying that our wounds are painful, denying that we feel weak, and denying that we are in need of comfort keeps God at a distance, the same way my niece kept me at a distance when I was trying to help her with her splinter. Healing won't happen until we let Him come close.

• • •

My senior year in college, I took eight weeks of writing courses in Harvard Summer School. It was my first visit to the historic institution, and I was not expecting the number of biblical references I saw in little nooks and crannies throughout the campus.

One discovery was a time-released revelation to me. On my way to classes each week, I had been passing Emerson Hall, the building that houses the philosophy department at Harvard. The enormous inscription above the front doors and columns of Emerson reads, "WHAT IS MAN." To me, it seemed an appropriate façade for a philosophy building.

Then one afternoon I happened to look up at the same moment that a heavy wind blew. The branches of a tree shifted to reveal that there was more to the inscription. The entire inscription reads, "WHAT IS MAN THAT THOU ART MINDFUL OF HIM." It is a verse from the Bible, the awed rhetorical question of King David in Psalm 8:4. And it is the most appropriate façade for *any* building because the only way to accurately view humanity is through God's eyes.

We are not in control, but God is. When difficulty strikes, we sometimes focus only on the first part of that thought: *We are not in control.* Our doubts and fears hang like tree branches over its conclusion.

I am not in control, I am not in control, I am not in control, we repeat in alarm, rehearsing the half-truths that unsettle us. The more we say it, the more our terror grows. If only we could walk in freedom instead of pacing back and forth in the captivity of incompletion and falsehood. No, we are not in control.

. . . *but God is.* That is always the rest of the sentence. But sometimes it takes a heavy wind in order for us to see it.

Another feature of the Harvard campus gave me chills. Harvard Yard is encircled by brick walls and twenty-five incredible gates, donated by graduating classes. The gates entranced me with their unique designs and inscriptions. One wrought-iron gate is particularly beautiful. It was donated by the Class of 1881, and at the top there is a cross, surrounded by a wreath, along with the words of Jesus as recorded in John 8:32, "And ye shall know the truth, and the truth shall set you free" (KJV).

The irony is astounding. That gate is *locked*. In fact, it has been locked for years.[3]

The same is true of a similar gate, just steps away. That one was donated by the Class of 1870 and stands just before lovely Holden Chapel, separating it from the grimy street traffic. Passersby can admire Holden's robin egg blue pediment, but they cannot get close to it.

Perhaps Harvard aims to preserve the gate itself or the beauty of the chapel by restricting too many visitors from the "outside." That is understandable, of course. But the spiritual application of the principle is also clear. Special places of worship certainly symbolize sanctity; they remind us that God is set apart as the Holy Other. But when we separate the worship of our hearts from the grit of our lives, we are imprisoned, locked away from the truth that would set us free.

We can't just go to church and forget to take God home with us.

Holiness came to a stable. He slept beside stinking animals. We do not have to keep Jesus clean. He had His own dark season. He knows how much a winter wound hurts, so we don't have to jerk away; we can let Him touch the painful places. Jesus the carpenter is no stranger to dirt and blood and . . . splinters.

I have learned, over time, to allow Jesus into the most difficult challenges in my life. I have stopped pretending that I have it all together. When I was twelve years old, I was diagnosed with systemic lupus, and at twenty years old, I suffered a massive brainstem stroke that almost killed me. Through rehabilitation, I learned to walk and talk again, but I live with the challenges of chronic illness and disability every day.

Some days just hurt, and when they do, I admit it. I used to think the Lord was disappointed in me when I didn't have enough faith to keep my own spirits up. Now I know I don't have to carry myself; He loves to carry me through my darkest moments. He wants to be there.

It doesn't matter if we are soiled with shame and defeat. It doesn't matter if we are filthy with defensiveness and indifference. He can begin with us the way we are. There is still time for healing, and there is still a way. But we have to let Him come closer.

God doesn't want to stay in our lovely chapels. He wants to walk the muck of our streets.

CHAPTER THREE

HE HAS A PLAN

The LORD *works out everything to its proper end.*

Proverbs 16:4

The Lord knows how to rescue godly people
from their trials.

2 Peter 2:9 NLT

THE SPEED OF MY ANSWER surprised me when someone recently asked, "What's next for you?"

"Obedience," I answered. "That's *always* what's next for me." Maybe I have finally learned that any other plan won't work.

Obedience is my plan.

Obedience was the plan for most of the tide changers in the Bible. This year I made a little project of marking certain themes in the Bible with certain colors. I am a sucker for school supplies, especially supplies in coordinated colors. It has crossed my mind that one reason I became a public school English teacher was to have a valid excuse to buy new school supplies every fall.

Newly armed with a set of highlighters in eight colors and a set of matching page tabs, I set out to annotate what I read in the Bible each morning. I marked passages that related to teaching. I marked passages that related to speaking and writing. I marked passages that related to handling adversity. And I marked passages that related to bearing fruit.

Immediately I realized that I also needed to highlight all of the passages that related to obedience, because there were many. I didn't mark the places that just mentioned the word *obedience*; rather, I marked the fantastic and miraculous stories that came about only because someone had obeyed. A basic example of this would be Noah. If he had not obeyed God's instructions to build a boat, his entire family would have been lost in the flood, and God would have used someone else to repopulate the earth. Actually, there is no simple way to imagine the outcome of his disobedience. It would have been catastrophic.

So as I labeled the traces of obedience in the Bible, page after page after page were awash in neon color. Florescent tabs stuck out like porcupine quills. Here is what I noticed in all of those stories: God unfolds His plan *after* the person takes a step of obedience, not before.

God does not fully explain to Abraham *how* a great nation will come through him. He just asks him to move to a new land. The plan unfolds *after* he does.

God does not fully explain to Moses *how* the Israelites will leave Egypt and escape Pharaoh with his pursuing chariots. He just asks Moses to approach the Red Sea. The plan unfolds *after* he does.

God does not fully explain any plan to anyone, as far as I can see in Scripture. He only asks them to do something. And *then* the plan unfolds.

An unfortunate truth also applies here. God does not fully explain to Eve that thousands of years of horror will come from eating the forbidden fruit. He just asks her *not* to eat it. We will never know how His original plan would have unfolded if she had obeyed. God's plan cannot be thwarted. But for now, the blueprint of heaven awaits.

What if God's best for our lives hinges on a step of obedience?

There is no better example of a destiny delayed by disobedience than in Numbers 13 and 14, when Moses sends twelve spies, one from each tribe in Israel, to scout out Canaan. This is the Promised Land that the Lord has said He will turn over as an inheritance to the Israelites. All the spies have to do is evaluate everything they see and return to the camp with a survey of the area. They are not supposed to go looking for an answer because there isn't a question about whether the Israelites will be successful in their mission to overtake the land. God has already said it will be so.

After forty days of scouting, the twelve spies return with conflicting intelligence reports. Two spies say that conquest is certain. They agree with God. Ten others argue, saying that the invasion will fail miserably. People throughout the camp become afraid. They believe the majority of the spies and do not believe God's promise. Jehovah has directed them to go into the land and take it, but the people are too scared to take action. They do not move forward; they just stand still and worry. It looks as if they are doing nothing, but the Lord says they *are* doing something. What they are doing is disobeying. As a result of this bald-faced rebellion, they secure a terrible consequence. God tells Moses,

> But as surely as I live, and as surely as the earth is filled with the LORD's glory, not one of these people will ever enter that land. They have all seen my glorious presence and the miraculous signs I performed both in Egypt and in the wilderness, but again and again they have tested me by refusing to listen to my voice. They will never even see the land I swore to give their

ancestors. None of those who have treated me with contempt will ever see it.[1]

The ten spies who disobeyed through disbelief are struck with a plague and die on the spot. The Lord sentences all of the rest of the Israelites to wander in the wilderness for forty years—one year for every day that the spies had scouted the land. Then the entire nation walks and walks and walks, taking a forty-year trip that would have taken only eleven days under normal circumstances.[2] Everyone over the age of twenty at the time of the spies' report dies without seeing the land of promise.

Except two.

Joshua and Caleb, the only spies who trusted God and returned from the scouting trip with positive news, are allowed to enter the land of Canaan. Did you notice they get the reward just for *intending* to obey and for encouraging others to do the same? They had not yet had a chance to do the actual work of obedience. It was all about their willingness and belief.

But one particular aspect of the story is most convicting to me.

In Numbers 14:3, when the Israelites hear the negative reports from the spies, they whine, "Why is the LORD taking us to this country only to have us die in battle? Our wives and our little ones will be carried off as plunder!" (NLT). We see that their justification for disobedience is concern for their children. They don't trust God with what is most precious to them.

Later, Moses gives the people this ironic decree, straight from God: "I will give the land *to your little ones*—your innocent children. You were afraid they would be captured, but they will be the ones who occupy it."[3]

The Israelites want to *protect* their children, while God wants to give *promise* to their children. His plans for us are much better than safety. But admit it, there are days when our own plans stop right there.

We all have our "babies," those things in our lives that are most precious to us—our health, our careers, our spouses, our dreams, our children. How many times have I withheld something I loved—my "baby"—trying to avoid tragedy, when the whole time God was trying to bring triumph in that very area?

My friend Becky tells of a day when she was in a minor car wreck while her infant was in the backseat. When she and the other driver tried to exchange insurance information, she had a challenging time balancing her son while she wrote.

"Here, I'll hold the baby," the man said.

"Thank you, but I can do it," she answered, continuing to write.

"It would go a lot faster if you would just let me hold the baby," he asked again.

"I appreciate your help, but I'd rather hold him," she said. He asked one more time before my friend turned to him and said, "Please do not ask me again. I only allow people I know to hold my baby."

She immediately saw the spiritual truth in what she had said. We only feel comfortable handing over our babies to someone we know. The same is true of our interaction with God. If we make the effort to know Him well, we will be more willing to hand over our "babies" to Him.

When God speaks to us, we must listen, believe, and obey, even if He asks us to turn over something that is precious to us. Belief is the all-important second step after listening because we will not obey if we do not take the time to consciously believe. The Message translates Ephesians 2:2 in terms of respiration, as if there is a spiritual by-product of what we breathe in: "You filled your lungs with polluted unbelief, and then exhaled disobedience."

On the other hand, this is healthy spiritual respiration: Breathe in belief; breathe out obedience.

God has a plan that is better than our plans. It may be tempting to think the people in the Old Testament had it easier in the way of hearing God. We assume He spoke to most of them directly and audibly in order to reveal a new assignment. True, He often sent an angel to communicate with them. These days, we may feel at a disadvantage. When we need an answer about something specific, the communication can seem a little murky. We wish He'd show up in a blaze of fire or send an angel to tell us in person.

Do you need an example of a hope hunter in the Old Testament who receives her task much the way we receive ours today? Take Ruth. God does not speak to her the exact way He spoke to Abraham and Moses and many others. She does not see a miraculous sign or a celestial being. For Ruth, her step of obedience begins as an urge of the heart that she can't shake. No one explains to her that King David will be her great-grandson if she will put aside her own possibilities for a future family and support her embittered mother-in-law. She just knows it is the right thing to do. And so she takes an obedient step toward relationship, not knowing where it will lead. God notices the way she chooses humility and puts others before herself. The plan that He unfolds as a result of her obedience is nothing short of a regal reward. Not only is she in the lineage of King David, she is in the lineage of King Jesus. God gives back a better family than the family Ruth was willing to give up for Him.

In addition to Ruth, there is Esther, an extraordinary hope hunter whose status as a member of the royal house makes it obvious that she must take a step of obedience to save the Jews from annihilation. Again, there is no ray of light, no earthquake, no disembodied voice. It is the advice of a mentor that guides her. A godly relative whom she loves and trusts directs her toward the path she should take. No one tells her whether the Jews will die or whether she will die. Esther is willing to take an obedient step into the throne room, not knowing how it will end. The plan that God unfolds as a result of her obedience not only saves her, it saves an entire population. Her people are no longer threatened, there is no longer a traitor in their midst, her dearest relative is brought into the palace, and she enjoys a closer relationship with her husband. God gives back a better life than the life Esther was willing to give up for Him.

It is essential to remember that both of these women are well into their personal winters when they are asked to take a step. Ruth is newly a widow. Esther has just discovered the plot for a genocide. Days are dismal. Wind whips their hearts, and there is no hope on the horizon. This is how they begin the hunt—with nothing in hand. God does not spare them the hard work of the search. The steps of obedience they take are steps into spring. But God does not explain that. No, He just asks them to start walking.

• • •

When circumstances are difficult, that is the time for you to start walking. But first, you must stop and be still. Strip away all the things that are keeping you from seeing the next step. One way to do this is by fasting. If you have a heart urge that you think may be direction from the Lord, set aside time to pray and fast. That is what Esther does. She and her people fast for a set period of time. Before she takes a step that could end her life, she wants to make sure it is a step that God Himself is asking her to take. Praying and fasting are ways that we cooperate with God's plan. He is the best collaborative partner we will ever have, and if we want to make sure to get His input in a situation, we should ask Him for it.

The bigger the step and the higher the stakes, the more important it is to include fasting with your inquiry. If this step of obedience would significantly affect life as you know it, then fast in order to discern His will.

About discernment, Paul writes, "Do not conform to the pattern of this world, but be transformed by the renewing of your mind. Then you will be able to test and approve what God's will is—his good, pleasing and perfect will."[4] The "pattern of this world" is to do things independently, to make decisions based upon what appears logical. But that is not the pattern of heaven. The pattern of heaven is best described as upside down, for "God chose things the world considers foolish in order to shame those who think they are wise. And he chose things that are powerless to shame those who are powerful."[5]

Things are not what they seem.

Jehovah says, "As the heavens are higher than the earth, so are my ways higher than your ways and my thoughts than your thoughts."[6]

Then how can we discern a will so high above us? We must bow low. We approach Him in extreme humility, not even attempting to know the direction we should take. We humble ourselves by fasting.

In one of the most eye-opening stories in the Bible, Daniel is devastated by some news and begins to pray about it. Not only does he pray about it, he fasts from choice food and wine for three weeks. And the result? A warrior angel comes to his aid.

"Do not be afraid, Daniel," the angel says. "Since the first day when you set your mind to gain understanding and to humble yourself before your God, your words were heard, and I have come in response to them."[7] Gabriel goes on to explain that he is three weeks late in arriving because he has been fighting evil forces in the heavenlies. By seeking

God humbly through prayer and fasting, Daniel has been engaging in spiritual warfare. But he doesn't know it until then.

Fasting is a necessary part of prayer because it humbles us like no other action we could take. I fast from food sometimes, but another effective way that I fast is by refraining from something else I enjoy. This can allow for a longer period of fasting than is possible with food. A few times I have fasted from music in the car for forty days. I love to listen to music while I drive. When music is absent, I really miss it. I might even miss music more than I would miss food! When I am fasting this way, I use all my driving time to pray. (With my eyes *open*, of course.)

Before you take a big step of obedience:

1. If you are married, talk to your spouse. Many times God confirms steps of faith quickly through this relationship. You might even consider praying and fasting from something together as a family. If you are not married, talk with another prayerful mentor or friend you respect.

2. Commit to a time of fasting. Depending on your health and situation, fast only a day or two from food, or fast as much as forty days from another

activity you will be hungry for. Be creative when you approach fasting.

3. Use the time you would normally be doing that activity to pray and listen. Let His presence fill the day. In time, you will know where He is leading you.

You may be walking through winter, but God knows how many steps are left until you reach spring. Sometimes the cold won't end until you move to a warmer climate. Trust Him to take you there. There is no way to know the best place to settle our hearts, so we have to ask God and then act on what He says. God is an expert at devising intricate plans, therefore ours can be pretty simple: Obedience. That's what's next for all of us.

Start walking. If we want a miraculous deliverance, if we want to find a way out, we might have to approach the unknown. We might have to turn over our plans in favor of His plan.

We might have to get to know Him better so that we can trust Him to hold our babies.

CHAPTER FOUR

HE HEARS YOU

---

*The eyes of the L*ORD *are on the righteous, and his ears are*
*attentive to their cry; but the face of the L*ORD *is against*
those who do evil, to blot out their name from the earth.
*The righteous cry out, and the L*ORD *hears them;*
*he delivers them from all their troubles. The L*ORD *is close to*
the brokenhearted and saves those who are crushed in spirit.

Psalm 34:15–18

WHEN I WAS IN eighth grade, my mother managed to
save enough money to buy four tickets to the Ringling Bros.
and Barnum & Bailey circus. Our family had been through
crippling stress since my diagnosis with systemic lupus ery-
thematosus two years earlier, and my mother thought we
could use a day's diversion. For too long, we had been talking of kidney biopsies, immunosuppressant medications,
and chronic pain. She couldn't wait for us to have a fun
evening when we could focus on other things.

That Sunday night, we drive into Fort Worth to attend

the evening performance of the circus. On the way, my mother grows giddy. Her words are magic wands, conjuring anticipation for the legendary Gunther Gebel-Williams and his trained tigers. This doesn't affect me at first. I am in junior high, so I have firmly decided that "The Greatest Show on Earth" probably isn't all that great. Still, there is something about any live performance, and the nearer we come to the convention center, the more I feel caught up in the spell. I am spun in the wonder of a *real* circus. When we arrive, my father is surprised to find an empty parking space so quickly. My fifth-grade brother and I look at each other; by then, we are smiling. We can smell the roasted peanuts from the parking lot, can hear the trumpet of an elephant.

Then everything stops.

"Oh?" my mother says suddenly. All of us stare at her. She cocks her head as she looks at the people passing by, "What's this?"

Happy families pour out of the convention center by the hundreds: children clinging to cotton candy and neon bracelets, mothers dragging plastic souvenir cups and stuffed ponies, fathers carrying sleeping toddlers.

"The matinee must have just ended. The performers are probably going to get ready for the evening show very quickly," my mother mutters, but this doesn't sound right, and we all know it. A silence settles around us like in every scene of *The Godfather* trilogy right before the windows blow in. Mother gropes through her purse, casting aside wadded tissues and notes from Sunday sermons until she finds the four tickets.

Then she turns to us, her face a wide-eyed fury. "No, no, no! Nooo! Our tickets were for the *matinee,* not the evening performance! We missed the show! We missed it! It's over! We were supposed to be at the matinee!"

She stares at the tickets, and the smiles leave our faces. A circus calliope begins playing in my head, and suddenly it feels like *we* are the act in the center ring. Just a bunch of clowns in a tiny car.

We have missed the circus. Yet all of us know: there is still hope. This is because we know my mother is an artisan at asking questions. Her persistence has an elegant poignancy. Nothing stops her from trying. Not even worthless circus tickets. With a heaviness that weighs on her like cinder block shoulder pads, she leaves us behind in the car and walks into the convention center.

The audience has cleared out, but she heads in.

When she sees a hallway with a dim light, she turns that direction and finds an office with a couple of men discussing the last details of the night. She quietly knocks on the open door, and they invite her to enter. She explains why our family has not seen the show. She asks if there is any way we can transfer the tickets to another performance, maybe the following day.

"I am so sorry," one of the men says. "We are leaving Fort Worth tonight. There isn't another show here."

"Where is your next stop, then? If we can get there, may we see you at your next stop?" she begs, hoping it is Oklahoma City or Austin, somewhere close.

"We're going to Wichita."

They are leaving for Kansas. It is too far to justify a day trip.

"Is there any way I can get a refund for these tickets? Any way?" She holds out the tickets, with stubs still attached.

"I'm sorry, ma'am. That is not possible. I am truly sorry I cannot help you."

My mother swallows hard and walks back to the car. By the time she opens the door, she is crying. She stares out the window, morose the whole way home, and she doesn't tells us about that conversation with the circus manager. In fact, she does not discuss anything about that fateful evening at any time, but she carries those limp circus tickets in her wallet for a full year, grimacing every time she reaches for a dollar. This is not her strange penance.

It is because she is not finished.

Overwhelmed by a sense of guilt, she keeps reminding

herself that details matter, details matter, details matter. She promises herself she will make it right.

She watches for the billboards.

Eventually, they come. The circus returns to the Dallas/Fort Worth Metroplex the following year, and with shameless persistence, she picks up the phone.

Tears fill her eyes while it rings. She *has* to ask.

When someone answers, she requests a circus manager, and she holds her breath until he comes to the phone. Then she says, "Good afternoon, sir. Last year my family and I missed the circus because—"

"Oh, of course! I remember you!" He interrupts her that fast. There is a ringmaster's smile in his voice.

"Oh? Really?" She is surprised. "Um . . . That's great! Yes, I am the one who came and spoke with you afterward. Well, I thought I would call just in case there was a chance . . . because I still have those tickets, and—"

"I am *so glad* you called to check!" The circus manager chuckles. "I have an idea. Would you like to be my guest at the circus this year?"

"What?! Why, yes! Yes, we would!"

"That's perfect! Just go to the Will Call window this Friday for the show that begins at 7:30, okay?" he tells her. "Now, that's at *7:30 sharp*!" he repeats, laughing.

On Friday, we don't arrive on time. We arrive an hour

early. We pick up the tickets and—just like that!—our cheap, 365-day-old, nosebleed-section, far-to-the-left, all-my-mother-can-afford seats in Fort Worth's Convention Center are replaced by brand-new, heart-pounding, second-row, center-ring seats in Dallas's Reunion Arena. I am close enough to Gunther Gebel-Williams to kiss him. A clown hands my brother a blue balloon. It is, without question, the *greatest* show on earth. It is more than we deserve. It is more than we have dreamed.

In case you haven't figured it out, my mother is a hope hunter.

I'm not the only one who thinks so. The week after our circus trip, her tenacity earned her a brief write-up in the community section of the *Fort Worth Star-Telegram*. These days someone who just won't give up is newsworthy.

Now, a determined woman is not the kind of mother you want when you are trying to be cool in junior high, but it is exactly the kind you want when you are dying. Years later, when I was in a life-threatening situation after suffering a stroke, I knew from my bed in the intensive care unit that if this woman was willing to fight for a chance to see the circus, how much more would she fight for her daughter's life? Again and again, she asked God to spare me.

And He did.

By then, she had taught me that the key to getting any kind of decent answer is to ask the right person, at the right time, in the right way. When our hearts are beaten and our situations bleak, the right person to ask is always God. The right time to ask is always now. The right way to ask is always like a hope hunter—with shameless persistence. Ask for help simply, scream it if you have to, but don't waste any breath or time explaining *why* you need the help. God can see what's going on.

The Message presents Jesus' words in Luke 11:10 like this: "Don't bargain with God. Be direct. Ask for what you need. This is not a cat-and-mouse, hide-and-seek game we're in."

Jesus speaks those words right after He tells a strange story to teach his disciples the art of asking in prayer:

Suppose you went to a friend's house at midnight, wanting to borrow three loaves of bread. You say to him, "A friend of mine has just arrived for a visit, and I have nothing for him to eat." And suppose he calls out from his bedroom, "Don't bother me. The door is locked for the night, and my family and I are all in bed. I can't help you." But I tell you this—though he won't do it for friendship's sake, if you keep knocking

*long enough, he will get up and give you whatever you
need because of your* shameless persistence.

*And so I tell you, keep on asking, and you will
receive what you ask for. Keep on seeking, and you will
find. Keep on knocking, and the door will be opened
to you. For everyone who asks, receives. Everyone who
seeks, finds. And to everyone who knocks, the door will
be opened.*[1]

Shameless persistence. The NIV calls it "shameless audacity." I don't remember a single lesson in Sunday school
that taught me to pray with *shameless audacity.* But Christ
clearly encourages it. A few chapters later, in fact, He tells
another unsettling story.

*One day Jesus told his disciples a story to show that
they should always pray and never give up. "There
was a judge in a certain city," he said, "who neither
feared God nor cared about people. A widow of that
city came to him repeatedly, saying, 'Give me justice
in this dispute with my enemy.' The judge ignored her
for a while, but finally he said to himself, 'I don't fear
God or care about people, but this woman is driving
me crazy. I'm going to see that she gets justice, because
she is wearing me out with her constant requests!'"*

Then the Lord said, "Learn a lesson from this unjust judge. Even he rendered a just decision in the end. So don't you think God will surely give justice to his chosen people who cry out to him day and night? Will he keep putting them off? I tell you, he will grant justice to them quickly! But when the Son of Man returns, how many will he find on the earth who have faith?"[2]

Both of these stories make me squirm because they illustrate something about God that I do not understand. Sometimes He answers the first time we ask; sometimes He waits until we ask again. And again. And again.

But just because He lets us keep asking does not mean He has not heard or is not acting.

• • •

A couple years ago, my family went to the circus once more—a much smaller circus this time—so that my brother's kids could see the animals. My eldest niece was only four, and she sat in my lap. While the elephants performed, topped with ladies in sequined suits that shimmered like icicles in the spotlight, she leaned back and whispered to me.

"What are they going to do if the elephant poops?" she

asked, and before I could offer my best guess, the elephant nearest us lifted his tail and did exactly that.

My niece sat up straight and declared matter-of-factly, "Boom. It pooped."

We joked for days about her response and about how one minute she was asking a question, and the next minute it was happening. Now she's older, but we still use her phrase as a remark for stunning coincidences. For instance, if I come over to play with the kids, and one of us offhandedly says we are in the mood for spaghetti or soup or chicken fajitas, and then her mother walks into the room to say that she is making exactly what we mentioned, we will get so tickled.

"Boom-it-pooped!" we look at each other and say in unison.

Or if I am babysitting, and we are playing a game inside, I'll suggest that we go outside and draw with sidewalk chalk instead.

"Boom-it-pooped! I was *just* thinking we should do that!" my niece will say and laugh.

If only our prayers were answered that way. Wouldn't it be fabulous if we were *just* asking the Lord about our unemployment situation and then—*boom!*—the phone rings with a sure job lead? More often we have to wait awhile, toiling in prayer. Wise theologians have written many books insisting that God does not have to be pressed into acting on our behalf. Every time I read the Bible, I am more and more convinced that this is true. God does not need to be coerced into loving us and taking care of us any more than you have to be coerced into loving and caring for your own child. These stories of the hesitant friend and the reluctant judge are not about coercion. They intimate God's desire for us to come to Him, and often. He seeks to be in a lifelong conversation with us. Emergency prayers and all-in-one blasts in God's direction are just announce-ments, but conversations are ongoing. We are instructed to "pray without ceasing."[3] At times, our hard heads learn things the hard way. Christ is not one of those friends you catch up with every few months. Our communication with Him should be like breathing. You don't breathe only on Christmas and Easter. Or only on Sundays. Or only before you go to bed.

You breathe without ceasing.

• • •

If your brain has room for just one memorized verse from the Bible that will help you day to day, I say go ahead and make it James 1:6:

If you need wisdom, ask our generous God, and he will give it to you. He will not rebuke you for asking. But when you ask him, be sure that your faith is in God alone.[4]

If you memorize this one, then maybe you will remember that God is generous and wants us to ask Him for what we need. Asking God for help is not *our* idea. He invites our questions, and that may be the most comforting coat we have to cover ourselves with when we enter winter. If we are helpless, then we might as well ask for help. What else can we do?

It is important to note that sometimes His answer will be no, even after we have waited and asked and waited and asked. As I told you, my persistently praying mother asked God to spare my life, and His answer was yes. But she also asked Him to spare her father's, her mother's, and her brother's lives, yet they all died before she was thirty years old. Our great God is a mystery.

He hears you. May our mighty and mysterious God save us swiftly when we ask for help. And if His answer doesn't look the way we expect, may we have faith to worship Him anyway. The answer is not as critical as the asking, so ask. God will do something right away, but sometimes the first thing He does is give us remarkable peace to wait longer.

God never does *nothing* when we cry out to Him. So if you are wondering whether God acts on your behalf the moment you ask Him to . . .

Well, I think you know what my niece and I would say to that.

CHAPTER FIVE

HE CAN HANDLE IT

He does as he pleases with the powers of heaven and the peoples of the earth. No one can hold back his hand or say to him: "What have you done?"

Daniel 4:35

WE WENT CAR SHOPPING when I turned sixteen. There were plenty of sensible sedans littering the lot, but I was hoping we wouldn't walk toward any of those. I remember feeling excited when my father pointed to a pre-owned black Trans-Am, complete with the gold "firebird" spread wide on the hood.

"I can see you in that one." He laughed. "Let's try it."

I could picture myself in it too.

But the car salesman couldn't. "Wait. Are you sure she can handle something like this? I don't think you want this one," he said to my father, not hiding his doubt. I must have looked pretty inexperienced for a car salesmen to talk us *out* of buying a car.

We never turned the key. I think I only sat in the driver's seat for a few minutes before I admitted that the low angle and the long hood would be too tricky for me to maneuver. It was markedly different from our family's compact car that I had been practice driving in parking lots. I knew I couldn't handle a Firebird on the highway even before I felt the thunder of its engine.

But Jeff Gordon can handle it.

I laughed when I saw a Pepsi commercial featuring Jeff Gordon, champion NASCAR driver. The premise of the commercial is that Gordon, with his reputation and skill safely disguised by a goatee, glasses, and khaki jacket, would take a used car salesman on the test drive of his life.

Armed with a cache of hidden cameras, Gordon gets behind the wheel of a Camaro and feigns incompetence for a few seconds before he rips out of the sales lot and begins to race, speeding and spinning his way around an obviously closed course. The salesman/actor appears shocked in the video, bracing himself against the car door and screeching like a capuchin monkey.

At the end of the ride, the salesman jumps from the passenger seat and threatens to call the cops, just as his wild driver pulls off his fake moustache and declares, "I'm Jeff Gordon!"

The man is instantly relieved and grins as he says, "Wanna do it again?"

The commercial is not based in reality, but I saw some truth we can cling to: Jeff Gordon knows how to handle a car. The salesman's level of fear is directly proportionate to the perceived skill of the driver. When he thinks some yahoo is speeding on slick streets, he hollers obscenities and wants out. He shouts demands like, "Stop the car!" and threatens, "You are liable for any damages!" He curses and accuses the driver, calling him an "idiot." In the final seconds of the commercial, he yells, "Who do you think you are?"

But when the masterful driver reveals his identity, everyone applauds and laughs. Nothing is as bad as it seemed in the beginning. The moment the salesman discovers an expert driver is behind the wheel, he doesn't mind the ride.

Maybe our twists and turns with God are like that. The faster and wilder He drives us through life, the more we act like frightened passengers. We feel out of control and unsafe. But God never thinks, *Oh, wow. I haven't seen* this *before. I am not sure what to do here.* No sharp turn could catch Him by surprise. His navigational skill is unsurpassed. Does it change our perspective and level of emotion if we know the true identity and the expert credentials of the One behind the wheel?

I don't know that I have ever cursed at God or called

Him names, but I have certainly cried out to Him about my situation. My quiet time is not always quiet. At times I have hollered loud enough for heaven to hear, "My whole life is at stake! I hope You know what You're doing, Lord!" We are deeply afraid that He doesn't. The times my life has spun sickeningly out of control are the times I have just wanted to open the door and jump out. Some lasting bouts of depression have left me feeling like I didn't want to wake up anymore.

Everything pivots on one point: the Driver's expertise. We are safer in the car than out of it. We don't really want to throw open the door; we only want to see where He is taking us. And if we try to help or grab the steering wheel away, we'll make things worse. *We* are the ones who don't know what we're doing.

Hope is going to move fast, and sometimes hunting it will require acceleration. This may feel frightening on slick winter roads, but God knows how to drive. It doesn't matter how bad the conditions become. In fact, God's skill in handling the hairpin curves of the high-octane human race makes Jeff Gordon look like he's behind the wheel of a plastic Cozy Coupe.

And it makes us look like a kid with a beginner's permit behind the wheel of a Firebird. Life is really just too powerful for us to handle.

• • •

The champion of suffering is Job. After losing everything he owns, including his children and his health, he has some legitimate questions for God. But God has some questions of His own, all of which are designed to bring Job to the most important question. He begins with, "Brace yourself like a man; I will question you, and you shall answer me."[1] Then He offers a list that puts Job in his place, saying,

> *Have you entered the storehouses of the snow*
>   *or seen the storehouses of the hail,*
> *which I reserve for times of trouble,*
>   *for days of war and battle?*
> *What is the way to the place where the lightning is*
>   *dispersed,*
>   *or the place where the east winds are scattered*
>   *over the earth?*
> *Who cuts a channel for the torrents of rain,*
>   *and a path for the thunderstorm,*
> *to water a land where no one lives,*
>   *an uninhabited desert,*
> *to satisfy a desolate wasteland*
>   *and make it sprout with grass?*
> *Does the rain have a father?*
>   *Who fathers the drops of dew?*

From whose womb comes the ice?
Who gives birth to the frost from the heavens
when the waters become hard as stone,
when the surface of the deep is frozen?[2]

I'm pretty sure I don't ever want to hear God say, "Brace yourself, Nika." When He says it to Job, He is about to unveil a description of His might and Job's inadequacy at the same time. The questions He levels at Job are not harsh, just direct. All of Job's questions are based upon "why." All of God's questions are based upon "who."

The why never matters as much as the who. God tames the sea. Lightning reports to Him. He prepares a feast for the lioness. From His womb comes the ice. Nothing surprises Him. When you are facing a trauma that makes you ask why, reframe your question with who. The "who" can put the "why" into perspective. Knowing Who is in control will wrap peace around the "why."

Who should be behind the wheel? God. Instead of asking Him to allow you to regain some control of a hazardous situation, just let Him take over. He can handle it. Ask God to show up and be God.

Then brace yourself. You're in for the ride of your life.

CHAPTER SIX

HE HAS GONE BEFORE YOU

Blessed are you, Israel!
Who is like you,
a people saved by the LORD?
He is your shield and helper
and your glorious sword.

Deuteronomy 33:29

SUNDAY SCHOOL shortchanges kids sometimes. We present to our children the same cinematic Bible stories that we enjoyed when we were small. But just when the narrative gets really interesting, we zoom out and fade to black. That is certainly what we do with the story of David and Goliath. Before the tale truly ends, we leave the young shepherd still on the battlefield, with a hulk's head hanging in his hands. The story isn't over. In my opinion, the best part of this legendary account of boy versus beast happens later.

But I had never noticed it before.

The Bible is always new. Only something living is always new. God's Word is "alive and active."[1] It is forever fresh, flexible enough to meet any need.

Let me clarify: the Bible never evolves; God's Word stands through eternity. It is *flexible* in that it is as applicable in the life of a two-year-old as a ninety-two-year-old. Yes, but it does not adapt to us. It never changes. Because the Bible does not change, it is the one thing that can change us.

Isaiah hears God *loud* and clear on this point.

> *A voice said, "Shout!"*
> *I asked, "What should I shout?"*
> *"Shout that people are like the grass . . .*
> *The grass withers and the flowers fade,*
> *but the word of our God stands forever."*[2]

If God told a prophet to shout, then it must be something He really wants us to hear.

How can the Bible always be new *and* always be the same? Think of it this way: Because humans are alive, our bodies are constantly renewing at a cellular level, but we as persons are always the same. Touch my arm when I am forty, and you will not be touching the exact same skin cells I had when I was four, but you will still be touching the same person. Of course, that is an imperfect way of understanding the living quality of the Bible. But all we have are dust-bound, human ways of comprehending something that is entirely supernatural.

The renewing nature of the Bible surprised me when I saw the rest of the story about David and Goliath. This lovely detail had not appeared out of nowhere; I am sure I had read it many times. Yet, I think a season of difficulty played a role in helping me notice it for the first time. Perhaps it was the darkness of that situation that provided the perfect environment for me to see something new glowing in 1 Samuel 21.

In that chapter, David has long lost his historic sling-shot, and we find him seeking a bigger weapon. Years after slaying Goliath, he had enjoyed a time of favor in King Saul's sight, even working for a while as a palace musician. But those days are over. Now David is fleeing the jealous king *and* his royal army. David knows a shepherd's simple tools aren't going to cut it anymore. His enemy could catch up with him any minute, and he needs something for close combat.

He bursts into the tabernacle located in the city of Nob and does not tell the truth about his deadly relationship with King Saul. He lies to the priest, Ahimelek, saying that he has been sent by Saul on a royal assignment. He doesn't say he's running from Saul; he says he's running Saul's errand. Then he asks for something to eat. After his quick meal of sacramental bread, we eavesdrop on the conversation that I had overlooked all these years.

> David asked Ahimelek, "Don't you have a spear or a sword here? I haven't brought my sword or any other weapon, because the king's mission was urgent."
>
> The priest replied, "The sword of Goliath the Philistine, whom you killed in the Valley of Elah, is here; it is wrapped in a cloth behind the ephod. If you want it, take it; there is no sword here but that one."
>
> David said, "There is none like it; give it to me."
> (vv. 8–9)

I read this passage and lost my breath. How long has Goliath's sword been in the corner by the time David arrives?! The timing is exquisite. The Lord has gone before David and provided for him in an unexpected way. He knows what David needs before David knows what he needs. And God does not just provide the minimum. Never. He provides the incomparable.

"There is none like it," our warrior marvels. *None* like

it. I can see him opening the cloth cover of this legendary sword, his eyes shining. He realizes God has perfectly equipped him.

There's something even sweeter in this passage. God knows David's situation is so dark that he needs something else—an encouraging word straight from his Father's heart. God means Goliath's sword to be more than just equipment; it is empowerment. Instantly, David recognizes that weapon because he has wielded it before. That is the same sword he had used to decapitate the giant with one triumphant strike. Do you see what I see here? A weapon can't be owned by a dead man. To the victor belong the spoils. Priest Ahimelek is mistaken. That sword in the corner *isn't* Goliath's.

It is David's.

Isn't it like the Lord to remind us of past victories as we enter new territory? God used the memory of David's previous battle to empower him for the next.

In effect, Yahweh was saying, "Young shepherd, a deadly army is on your tail. You are the underdog, no doubt about it. But remember, you have been the underdog before. With Me, nothing is impossible for you. You may be pursued by a king, son, but the King of kings stands with you. Do not be afraid."

The best of our cinema isn't better than this. Can't you picture David's shoulders rising? Can't you hear the soundtrack's thundering crescendo as our hero pulls the ragged cloth from the sword? Light glints off the blade, and the future king remembers who he is.

Just like that, David is no longer someone being hunted. He is someone *on* the hunt. And when we see the set of his jaw, we know: He's on his way to hope.

No one equips—no one empowers—like our God.

• • •

When I looked up from this ancient story, I realized that it was applicable to my own life. Though my heart was facing a difficult battle at the time, God had gone before me. He had not provided in a minimal way either. He had provided in the best way, just as He has provided for you.

He has equipped us. Our sword is the Word of God.

Yes, Hebrews 4:12 tells us the Word of God is alive and active. But it also says that the Bible is "sharper than any double-edged sword."

In our "stand against the devil's schemes" we can arm ourselves with "the sword of the Spirit, which is the Word of God."[3]

We will have everything we need if we will read. Each time I have faced the enemy, I have come away with greater strength. My battles have become more and more challenging over the years, but my armory for spiritual warfare has always matched the battles in increasing potency. I go from strength to strength.

"Blessed are those whose strength is in you, whose hearts are set on pilgrimage" (Psalm 84:5). And verse 7 tells us, "They go from strength to strength, till each appears before Zion."

Seasons are not linear. We don't move straight through them and move on. Seasons are cyclical. Winter will come around again. In my life, I have noticed that dark seasons look different but often have the same theme.

One of my first great adversities was experiencing a massive brainstem stroke in my twenties. It left me quadriplegic, and when I learned to walk and talk again, I was glad that dark season was over. But years later, winter circled back.

I was in a very dark season that second time, but it wasn't medical, so I didn't see the similarities at first. I would pray and pray about the problem, but it just wouldn't move! I felt like I couldn't lift a finger to fix it. My life seemed stuck, immobile. After a while, those feelings felt strangely familiar. It was a long time before I recognized there is a theme of paralysis in my winters. But when I did, I also recognized that God had given me specific tools to combat the terror of physical immobility during that first winter long ago. The tools already belong to me. I just had to learn to use them for *every* immovable circumstance, whether in my career, relationships, finances, or whatever.

Is it possible that the dark seasons in your life have had similar themes? Ask the Lord to help you see what they are. Maybe yesterday has prepared you for today. Before you begin a battle, ask the Holy Spirit to show you the sword in the corner—the weapon or tool that already belongs to you.

If we submit to the Lord, we will move from strength to strength, empowered by every vanquished foe. Christ wins the war, and we walk away with the spoils. This is because every time we apply a new Scripture—when we wield it to slay a giant in our lives—it becomes ours. It becomes *ours. Ours!* Never again do we read that verse with the same intonation; never again does it lie dormant on the page. When we carry a fresh truth in our hearts, we have gained a weapon, and the enemy has lost one. He will not be able to assault us with the exact same tactics because we are wise to him now and will recognize his strategy. The things we used to fear no longer frighten us.

Why do we tend to forget that the Lord has been faithful to go before and provide perfectly? Why do we tend to forget that He has used our former battles to equip and empower us?

Well, we could ask that question of David.

The remainder of 1 Samuel 21 records his shocking loss of confidence. The same day he reunites with his own mighty sword, David leaves Nob and moves on to Gath, where royal advisors warn King Achish of his arrival in the city, trumpeting the shepherd's reputation for triumph in battle. Even though David has the advantage, he is "very much afraid of Achish king of Gath. So he pretended to be insane in their presence; and while he was in their hands, he acted like a madman, making marks on the doors of the gate and letting saliva run down his beard" (vv. 12–13).

Wait, *what*?!

Can you believe that the anointed future king of Israel is drooling and scratching the doorposts? Doesn't he know he has been preparing for this confrontation?

Where is that sword?!

Before we become critical of him, let's admit that we too have had many "cities of Gath." Try to think of David the next time you feel defeated by your day and hear yourself saying, "This is driving me crazy!" or "You make me insane!" or "I'm going nuts!"

Remember David in the city of Gath the next time you find yourself scratching and clawing for any relief you can find. It is far too easy to forget who you are.

The Lord has gone before you. He has prepared you

with spiritual weaponry to face this fight. Your past may have been heavy, but God has used your yesterdays to strengthen you for today.

We have everything we need. But the Word of God won't do us much good in the corner, wrapped up, unused.

If we want a sword to take into combat, we'll have to open its cover.

CHAPTER SEVEN

HE IS WITH YOU

On my bed I remember you;
I think of you through the watches of the night.
Because you are my help,
I sing in the shadow of your wings.

Psalm 63:6–7

THE DRIVE TO SEMINOLE, Texas, is a lonely one. It is six hours of two-lane highway from my home in Fort Worth, but still, I decided to drive instead of fly to the women's conference that weekend. Because I would be speaking at the conference, I needed a clear head and clearer heart, so I sought some time alone to think through a few problems that were nagging at me. The issues were so frustrating, I hardly knew how to put words to my thoughts, hardly knew how to pray. So I chose to begin my trip by singing along with a praise CD, and before I began, I did something I had not done before. I moved everything that typically fills my passenger seat to the backseat. Then I hand swept the crumbs from the empty seat and prayed, "Lord, this is going to be a long drive. Please sit beside me the whole way as I sing to You. Be my guest of honor on this trip." I guess I said it symbolically, as a way of centering my thoughts on Him. It became more than a symbol.

Three hours into the drive, I still wasn't ready to stop singing, though I was going hoarse. Four hours in, the towns and traffic fell away, and dry mesas rose from the dusty horizon. I drove for miles without seeing another person, animal, or vehicle. Still, I sang louder. Five hours in, I lost cell phone reception. As far as I could see in every direction, the landscape was entirely flat, without so much as a spray of mesquite. Sure, it crossed my mind that it was dangerous to be in such a remote location without communication, but I wasn't worried. Songs filled the space, and the peace in my car was overwhelming. Usually, I am so tired at the end of a long road trip that all I can do is fall in bed for a nap, but this time the six hours felt like two. I arrived at the conference feeling remarkably refreshed.

I cannot explain how much I looked forward to getting back in the car to head home the next day. It wasn't because there was a problem with the conference. On the contrary, it had been an incredible event, one of the best I have experienced. I was on the verge of tears the whole time, awed by the faith and genuine warmth of the Mennonite women who welcomed me into their community to share a message for the weekend.

After the conference, I packed up my belongings, headed to a last-chance Dairy Queen before leaving town, and blasted the praise music for the long drive home. Just as I had hoped, a transcendent peace filled the car again, and soon my cheeks hurt from smiling for hours. The long drive was almost going too fast.

"Lord, why is this trip different from every other trip I have taken?" I said aloud. "Why are You so close and Your presence so tangible today?"

In my heart I heard clearly, "Draw near to me, and I will draw near to you."[1]

It is a verse I had read many times. In that moment, the written Word of God became the whispered Word of God. So often, God answers me by bringing Scripture to my mind.

When we open our hearts to the Lord, He opens our ears to hear Him. Why was His presence deeply felt on that trip to west Texas? I think He filled my car because I invited Him. Of course, God is always with us, always within us. However, when we intentionally host His presence, as we would a dear guest, He manifests Himself in new ways. We will see Him when we look for Him. We will hear Him when we listen for Him. We will sense Him when we make space for Him. On that trip, I had made actual space for Him in the passenger seat. But it was only symbolic of the figurative space I was making for Him in my thoughts. He will fill the entire space we make for Him. If there are times when we do not sense the fullness of His presence, we should ask ourselves if we have made enough space.

On beautiful days, we easily can feel Him near. We gaze on the bloom of a sunset, we breathe the perfume of a baby's skin, and we sigh, "Thank You, Lord." During our dark seasons, however, it is hard to believe He is there.

An ambulance rushed me to the intensive care unit only moments after my stroke, and there I would know days of greater physical and emotional pain than I thought I could endure. I was unable to move. Unable to speak. To blink. Around me, physicians spoke of nightmares, warning that I had forty-eight hours left to live. Predicting that if I lived at all, I would remain in a vegetative state. They warned my mother she might never hear her daughter say another word.

I couldn't speak, but I could hear. And when I heard that prognosis, I felt alone.

Rehabilitation helped me gain some basic movement and ability, but the darkness was far from over. My central nervous system had turned against me in a sudden betrayal. My sense of touch could not be trusted. Soft fabric felt like splintered wood. What was weightless felt heavy. Heat felt cool. Without warning, my arms and legs would sizzle or tingle or ache or go numb.

Sensation wasn't the only loss. Emotion had no order, and memory had no shape. When I heard tragic news, I laughed; humorous stories started me sobbing. All my feelings kicked loose from the reigns and bolted in chaos. My body was out of my control.

I couldn't remember how to tie my shoes. Couldn't remember how to swallow.

Even after rehabilitation, I wasn't myself. I left the hospital with slurred speech that would eventually improve and a limping gait that would not. Years later, I still use a cane on good days and a walker on bad ones.

Knowing death has changed the way I know life.

It is hard to accept the idea that God was there in my winter. Yet recently I asked Him to show me where He was on that day when so many of my dreams died. He was faithful to answer through a vision. In my mind's eye, I could see myself there, resting deeply the night before my dark season began. I wrote of the scene in my journal:

It is the sleep before suffering begins, and God leans low to watch me breathe, to speak into my peace. He watches my chest fill with the very breath He breathed into Adam. He sees my lashes flutter, and

He smiles like any father who stands over his sleeping child. A quick grin flies across my mouth too: a dream or sweet memory from the day. I cough and turn, feeling the breeze of the fan and pulling the bedsheets close around my neck. Sleep deepens, and I never know how near He is. Then with a gentle hand, God touches His fingers to my face. His love becomes agony.

Tomorrow, He whispers, pain in His eyes. *Tomorrow, when it happens, I will be with you.*

God at my bedside. The thought came to me for the first time when I read Psalm 139, a psalm of David. There, Israel's king sings,

O LORD, you have examined my heart
  and know everything about me.
You know when I sit down or stand up.
  You know my thoughts even when I'm far away.
You see me when I travel
  and when I rest at home.
  You know everything I do.
You know what I am going to say
  even before I say it, LORD.
You go before me and follow me.[2]

Wade deeper into the truth that God knows *everything* in advance, and our bedsides are exactly where we find Him. Not in some far heaven, but here with us. Here with me. Here with you.

Was this imaginative moment of the Lord by my bedside a vision from God or was it written by my own mind? The question of authorship is an old merry-go-round. Many artists have difficulty discerning the two in their work as well. Doesn't the Lord provide skill for and inspire every work of art attempted by one who is committed to Him? Can we take credit for any of them? If I have written a book or a letter that has touched someone deeply, I must ask: Did I do it, or did God do it through me? Only He would know just what to say.

There are times when He surprises us with a word or picture that we sense as distinctly from Him, but when we are spending time with Him intentionally—actively asking Him to speak—then our hearts are in communion with Him. The more we commune with Him, the more difficult it is to distinguish His initiatives from our own. We become like Him. His desires become ours. Our minds, like His. He moves the artist's brush and the writer's pen.

And He will illustrate our life story if we ask Him to. He can reveal to us a better picture of our past.

If we show the Holy Spirit some hospitality, He starts

the healing process in our memories. In fact, you can see it there, right within the word *hospitality*: *hospital*. If I am aching over adversity or doubting God's loving attention, I ask Him to show me how He really views me and the trials I have faced. I ask Him to show me where He was and where He is. He can seem so far removed, so silent at times. The winter experiences of our lives leave us feeling very alone, indeed. He is near, but it can feel dark and quiet, even in the shadow of His wings. Especially there. I have to deliberately believe what He says, not how I feel, and He *says*, "Be sure of this: I am with you always, even to the end of the age."[3] It doesn't matter if I *feel* alone; that is never the truth. So, sometimes I dare to ask God where He was on the day—at the moment—that winter blew in. Then I wait in snowy silence. He always answers. His answer always heals.

Not long ago, I took one of my most painful childhood memories to Him. When I was five years old, an adult I loved and admired had misunderstood my childlike behavior in a situation and had accused me of having sinister motives.

The spiteful words that were spoken to me that day had been wounding me for thirty-five years, but I had never spoken to God about it. That memory would pop up every once in a while, especially when something current seemed to contribute to or reinforce those old words.

"Maybe it is true," I would consider. "Maybe I *am* all of those things."

I was tired of thinking about the sting of that day, tired of seeing the same sad scene in my mind, tired of hearing the same cruel insults. I already knew what *I* thought about that memory. But wasn't it one of God's memories too? I wanted to know what *He* thought about it, how *He* remembered it. My whole life, I had effectively left Him out of the mental discussion of that heartache, never talking to Him about an incident I was so painfully tied to. I was acting like He wasn't part of it. But I knew that wasn't true.

"Where were You that day, Lord? Where?" I called to Him, tears filling my eyes.

My mind reviewed the memory as I had always seen it, but this time there was something new and unexpected. I wasn't alone. Jesus was sitting beside me. I had never pictured it that way before.

He was *there* that day.

The memory continued. That person from my past spun around to face me and squeezed my hand tighter and tighter, crushing the ice cream cone I held in my tiny fingers, spitting the accusations I had replayed two million times, but this time I saw Jesus wince as every heavy word hit my heart. As I was hurt, He was hurt. Tears were in *both* of our eyes.

Seeing and sensing His presence in that situation gave me strength to do something I had never done before, something that I should have done years ago. Courage welled up in me, and I gave words to it.

"I . . . I . . . I choose to forgive," I said out loud for the first time. Maybe I had just wanted someone to ache for the younger me—to ache for that little girl's heart—so that she wouldn't be aching alone. Jesus was letting me know that all these years He had been aching for that little girl, so I no longer had to be the one to do it.

I cannot explain the healing that took place in my heart in an instant. In an *instant*! The memory is still there, of course. We can't wipe away our lives. However, the hurt associated with the memory is completely gone. I no longer ruminate over that event, because there is no pain that needs to be soothed anymore.

We don't need to fear opening the past to God. It is not risky or frightening. He will not take our hearts into dangerous places. He will always lead us toward healing. No matter where He takes us, He will always bring us back whole. We can "pour out [our] heart[s] like water before the face of the LORD."[4] He is the Wonderful Counselor.

I am a visual learner, so I really "get it" when I can see it. It is a good thing our God can teach with various methods. He is colorful and creative; every brilliant thing that exists was born of His imagination. And because we are made in His image, we possess His powerful inner eye. No wonder He often communicates with His people in dreams. When He ignites our imaginations, He is using one of His favorite teaching tools.

My inner eye helps me understand God so much better that I invite my imagination into my quiet hour daily. There is no reason to lock this vibrant part of my mind outside the prayer closet door. Some people have never experienced what they consider to be a "vision" from God, but we *envision* things we desire every day. If you have ever pictured yourself enjoying the vacation you are planning, then you already know how to do this. In fact, if you have ever caught yourself daydreaming at all, you are already an expert at envisioning.

A Spirit-led and fertile imagination—grown from the seeds of the Living Word—brings healing in beautiful ways. It could be that one way you must hunt for hope is to look for it in your past. Can you envision the truth that God knew about the dark seasons of your life before you did? What would that look like? Identify the recent upheaval, the blow, the trauma, the wound, the diagnosis that woke you from the sweet dreaming of your days. Then consider for a moment that God was there in the fullness of that event. He saw the shape of it, felt the weight of it, could hear it almost breaking you. He knew the size of the wreckage before you were born. And He knew, even then, that He was going to walk into it with you.

The night before your world changed, you had been busy about your day with an effortless smile, laying your tired body down to rest that evening. Moonlight spilled from the windowsill. You straightened the folds of your quilt, felt the coolness of the pillow, heard the purr of the fan. Your breathing slowed to the even pattern of sleep.

Then the Lord knelt beside your bed, looking on with tenderness.

He knew what would happen tomorrow. He knew your heart would be broken. He knew that the phone call would come during breakfast or that the accident would happen in the afternoon. He knew how your doctor would phrase it or how your boss would explain it away. He knew where you'd be when you picked up the note and how it would feel in your trembling hand. He knew what you would find on the screen. He knew what you would see when you opened the door.

He knew that this would be the last night you would sleep for many, many nights ahead.

With a gentle hand, He touched your face.

Tomorrow, He whispered, pain in His eyes. *Tomorrow, when it happens, I will be there with you.*

CHAPTER EIGHT

HE IS CHANGING YOU

Anyone who loves their brother and sister lives in the light,
and there is nothing in them to make them stumble.
But anyone who hates a brother or sister
is in the darkness and walks around in the darkness.
They do not know where they are going,
because the darkness has blinded them.

1 John 2:10–11

I REMEMBER THE DAYS before I was a hope hunter. The keenest memory of it almost makes me laugh and cry simultaneously. I was eighteen years old and blinded by depression.

There should have been a warning siren. An emergency radio signal interruption. There should have been an oversized highway sign to alert me to the darkness ahead:

Now Leaving Fort Worth
Now Entering Winter

There wasn't. I drove a packed Chevy Blazer—filled to the ceiling with clothes, framed posters, and bed linens— to my orientation week at college. I was oblivious to the heartache I'd brought along as well. As I switched lanes on I-20, I remember asking myself if I had brought enough necessities and mementos from home. I should have been asking myself if that was *all* I was bringing.

The first day was enjoyable, I'm sure. Maybe the second too. By the third or fourth day, however, a soul-wasting pain had leeched into my bones, weakening my confidence and leaving me without strength to breathe. Weeks later, my mother choked with concern when I called home and told her I hadn't eaten in three days. I was too hurt to be hungry, my heart too broken to lift a fork. I didn't tell her I hadn't attended class in twice as long.

I was still going to work, but my appearance reflected despair. I dressed appallingly at my job as a student worker, where I answered phones in the administrative offices of the university. The student worker in the room next to mine wore a skirt and kitten heels. I wore stringy cutoff jeans and Converse shoes without socks. She smelled like French perfume. I smelled like french fries. She greeted visitors to the office of the provost, looking capable in her smart blouse. I greeted visitors to the office of the president looking pitiful in my band T-shirt. Yes, I worked in the office of *the president of the university.* Why they did not fire me and boot me back to the dorm, I'll never know. I think they might have been waiting for me to flunk out, which seemed inevitable.

I spent all the rest of my time in bed. My emotions were complicated by another devastating fact. I had been on chemotherapy—a treatment for lupus—for five months before I left for college. By the time I got there, I was bald, still sick, and completely spent.

Buried under the covers on many days, I missed both social opportunities and assignment due dates, finally earning mediocre to low grades in all subjects. I had a full-blown F in history, solely due to the fact that I never had enough energy to show up for class . . . or even to withdraw with the registrar.

A friend stopped by my room to wake me each morning.

Monday: She shook my shoulders. "Come on! Get up. Let's go! I'm not gonna let you stay like this much longer!"

Tuesday: She opened the curtains. "See all those people outside the window? The ones wearing backpacks? They're going to class, which is what *you* are supposed to be doing right now."

Wednesday: She threw a pillow at my head. "Hey! A group of us are going out to eat tonight. It'll be fun! Don't stay in bed."

Thursday: She opened the door. I rolled over, pulling the blanket over my face. She sighed and left.

Friday: She didn't come.

I didn't know how to eject myself from a plane on its way down. I was hurtling to the ground as the fuselage of my future twisted and tore at the seams. I didn't want to be away at college, but I didn't want to be back at home either. I was depressed for the first time, and if I had known how to stop the nosedive, I would have.

The crash had been coming for a while. Even an airplane needs regular maintenance and equipment checks before a flight, but sometimes we offer much less detailed attention to ourselves. We take off on new adventures without routine upkeep and care. If we don't schedule simple heart checks with friends, mentors, or counselors, it is only a matter of time until there's an emergency.

I had let the ache go for too long . . . I had let the ache *grow* for too long. And I had brought it with me to college. Two years before, when I was in high school, my father had left our family, and my mother had experienced a lot of added responsibility. I had been close to my father, and became so hurt and resentful in his absence that I was cold to my mother, blaming her for his decision to leave. I didn't even want to hug or touch her. However, she had begun a spiritual awakening in the aftermath of our family's upheaval, so she was gentler and more affectionate than ever before. She had never been one to cry much, so I didn't know how to react to the tears I saw in her eyes more often. The warmer she became, the colder I became.

Back then, my irritation progressed to the point that I couldn't tolerate time at home. I felt bitter and angry and trapped, classic signs of unforgiveness.

When my father moved out, my younger brother went to live with him, so that left my mother and me to swirl through the rooms of our house like warm and cold air currents. Every time we came in contact with one another, naturally, there was a tornado. I couldn't wait to get away.

It is easy to idolize an imagined relief. I remember thinking about the imagined relief of college life all the time. My fantasy looked like this:

- *In college*, I will do whatever I want without having to argue every day.
- *In college*, I will live with friends who are happy, and I will be happy.
- *In college*, all of those happy friends will love me unconditionally.
- *In college*, I will maintain my happy relationship with my happy boyfriend, who will never leave me like my father did.

- *In college*, I will fit into my cute jeans. (Always on the list.)

You know what *really* happened when I got to college, of course, because you have experienced your own version of imagined relief before. I shall now examine my list of expectations in light of reality.

First Expectation—*In college, I will do whatever I want without having to argue every day.*

Well, let's see. My version of "doing whatever I want" involved eating two cans of Spaghettios with meatballs for dinner seven days a week. I like the flavor of Spaghettios with meatballs better than the taste of plain Spaghettios, though I don't like texture of the meatballs themselves. That means I have to pick them out. (There is no need to discuss this; it will slow down the story. Let's move on, shall we?) As I said, I was depressed, with no energy at all, so I left bowls of meatballs stacked in the tiny dorm room sink until I ran out of bowls or decided to wash them on a random Saturday. It just so happened that dealing with a sink full of dirty dishes wasn't my roommate's version of "doing whatever *she* wants," so that kind of shot the whole "without having to argue every day" part of the plan.

Oh, how we argued.

Second Expectation—*In college, I will live with friends who are happy, and I will be happy.*

My roommate *wasn't* happy. Clearly.

But I was feeling so miserable and unmotivated that I wasn't sensitive to her feelings and I didn't stop adding to the plastic mountain of bowls each week. Repeatedly, my roommate explained her frustration and her desire for my habits to change. I mean, I *wanted* to change, really, I did . . . but if you have ever felt pinned to the wall by heartache, you know that you can't just get up because you decide to. Your spirit has to change. I would promise to improve, but within a few days I would be every bit as irresponsible as before.

We bickered badly one night, and when I remained stubborn in refusing to clean up our room sink, she took all of my bowls down the hall to the community bathroom, where there were eight huge sinks in a row. I told myself I would clean them out of there tomorrow. But there is a problem with tomorrow: it never comes.

By the end of the week, everyone on our end of the hall became involved. They were tired of dirty bowls in the sink. One night I woke up at midnight needing to use the bathroom. I stumbled to the door of our room, took a step over the threshold, and felt my bare toes squish into meatballs. All of my bowls were piled on the floor outside the door. I froze, then looked up. A seven-foot banner hung down the hallway. I squinted my myopic eyes to read it slowly.

NIKA IS A PIG.

Every girl on Second Floor West had signed it.

Then *guess who* wasn't happy.

Third Expectation—*In college, all of those happy friends will love me unconditionally.*

As it turns out, they only loved me when I picked up after myself like a decent human being. I had no idea.

I hopped back into the room on my clean foot. My roommate pretended to be asleep, but I'd testify in court that she was smiling. I wiped my foot on my roommate's washcloth and then scooped up a roll of Scotch tape and two cans of Spaghettios with meatballs. I spent the next hour thinking about that banner while spooning out meatballs and taping them to the doorknobs of every room on my hall, as any mature person in pursuit of a college degree would do. I smiled, picturing each girl reaching for the doorknob and getting a squishy handful of canned meat.

I'm sure there is research somewhere that proves emotional trauma temporarily diminishes your IQ. See, it didn't occur to me until much later that my plot was poorly designed. The meatballs should have been on the *inside* doorknobs, not the outside doorknobs.

Details. Whatever.

Fourth Expectation—*In college, I will maintain my happy relationship with my happy boyfriend, who will never leave me like my father did.*

Let's be real. How long would *you* hang around a girl who picked out the meatballs from the two cans of Spaghettios she ate every night for dinner?

Fifth Expectation—*In college, I will fit into my cute jeans.*

Shut up . . .

The first moral of this story is: Thank the Lord we can change. I look back on myself at eighteen and shudder. It is not as if I am a totally different person today, but if there are times when my initial thought is an immature one, at least now I will exercise some maturity and not act on that thought.

The second moral of this story is: Wherever you go, there will be people. And you will have to get along with them. Now, in case you were wondering, my freshman roommate and I are still friends. We fought like sisters and loved one another like sisters; we've got stories that would keep you laughing for days. My problem wasn't her. My problem wasn't even my family, though I thought it was.

If your season of difficulty is the kind that involves a person or people you don't enjoy, you probably feel trapped and your imagined relief no doubt involves getting away from them. Be forewarned, no matter what person trap you are trying to escape, you are only going to head straight from *that* person trap into *another* person trap. You will *never* be able to release yourself. This is true for two reasons.

One, Satan does not want you to save yourself from anything. He never wants anyone to free you.

Two, God does not want you to save yourself from anything. He wants to be the One to free you.

And He knows a little secret: (shh) the *real* person trap is you.

Let me explain.

The New Testament is tricky. I've heard a lot of people argue that they like reading the New Testament better than the Old Testament. They claim that the New Testament has a fresher flavor and practical advice, while the Old Testament just has long lists and difficult names.

Me? I'm an Old Testament girl, myself. I love reading those wild adventures of people who would give up everything and blaze into battle, even *before* they knew Jesus! They were willing to act on just the hint of Him. Also—

I'll be honest—I like the long lists of rules in the Old Testament, probably because I am a classic firstborn child and feel an urge to mark off every last one of them. With color-coded pens. Check, check, check.

Then in the New Testament, the Messiah comes and messes with the lists.

He begins, "You have heard that it was said to the people long ago, 'You shall not murder, and anyone who murders will be subject to judgment.'"

Check! Not gonna murder anybody! I'm okay there, Jesus.

"But *I* tell you that anyone who is angry with a brother or sister will be subject to judgment."[1]

Are you *serious*?! Just *angry*? Now, Jesus . . .

Read on and discover other cool hits, like the command not to commit adultery (check!), which becomes a command not to lust (awkward silence).[2] And the hardest of all, where we used to get by with the oh-so-satisfying, eye-for-an-eye revenge on those who have hurt us (check!), now we have to turn our faces to them in forgiveness,[3] even if there is a chance we will be hurt by them again (crickets).

I have yet to check off a single list in the New Testament. Sure, I haven't murdered, but I have been angry. Very angry. I was so angry once I gritted my teeth and cracked my left molar. Trust me on this one: Stay calm and you will end up with the crown of life. Stay angry and you will end up with a crown on your tooth. I mean it.

Jesus warns that for anger, there is judgment. That's what's ahead. No wonder God will stop at nothing to help me put down my anger. He doesn't want me to "come to the judgment seat of Christ"[4] with fury still throbbing in my chest. His discipline in the meantime isn't to punish me; it is to prepare me for reward. That's what some dark seasons are for. Winter reveals weakness. Trials are not an abandonment, then, but a mercy. They give us another chance to change.

We have to trust God and stop trying to get out of our difficulties too soon, even by way of mental escape. Just as the command not to murder expanded to the command not to harbor anger, all of the Old Testament laws have expanded from hand to head. Well, really, to *heart*. For instance, you don't have to bow before a real idol anymore when a fantasy can be just as much of an idol to you. If you dream of deliverance every day, it may be damaging your spiritual fidelity. Each time we ruminate on imagined relief, we are fashioning an escape hatch with our own hands. The trouble is, any liberation system that is man-made is an idol. Resist the urge to lust after liberty. Just lean on God the Liberator.

In college, I felt trapped by my family situation, and I

thought I could escape it by moving to another town. But debilitating depression followed me because I had opened the door to the enemy through bitterness, anger, and unforgiveness toward my parents. Before I knew it, I was in a dark prison, indeed.

It is a comfort to know that nothing can happen to us without God's permission, even circumstantial incarceration. He will release us when we are ready for release. God freed Paul and Silas from jail by an earthquake. He freed the Israelites from bondage by splitting the sea. So if He wants to free us, He knows how. He doesn't need any of our puny getaway plans. Shaken earth and severed seas should tell us that when God sets free, He does it big.

But He knows that just because we are freed, it does not mean that we are free.

His heavenly wisdom defies human logic. God wants to change us into soul-free people *before* we are freed from our circumstances. A picture of this is painted in Psalm 107:10–16 (NLT):

> *Some sat in darkness and deepest gloom,*
> *imprisoned in iron chains of misery.*
> *They rebelled against the words of God,*
> *scorning the counsel of the Most High.*
> *That is why he broke them with hard labor;*

they fell, and no one was there to help them.
"Lord, help!" they cried in their trouble,
  and he saved them from their distress.
He led them from the darkness and deepest gloom;
  he snapped their chains.
Let them praise the Lord for his great love
  and for the wonderful things he has done for them.
For he broke down their prison gates of bronze;
  he cut apart their bars of iron.

And again in Micah 7:8–9:

Though I have fallen, I will rise.
Though I sit in darkness,
  the Lord will be my light.
Because I have sinned against him,
  I will bear the Lord's wrath,
until he pleads my case
  and upholds my cause.
He will bring me out into the light.

If, in our stubbornness, we do not accept the mandate to forgive, then it doesn't matter how far away from imprisoning situations we run, we remain under lock and key. Unforgiveness is rebellion against the Word of God, and there is a natural consequence: a season of darkness. Forgiveness keeps us in the light; unforgiveness keeps us in the dark. And God will let us live in it until we finally admit we are willing to do things His way. If we choose to cry out to God and ask for His help to forgive, then it doesn't matter how dark the prison cell of our condition; getting out doesn't seem quite so important anymore. We are *immediately* soul-free. Circumstantial freedom may follow.

There may be an even deeper root in your heart than unforgiveness, and only the Lord can tell you what it is. So many times, we do not realize that we are opening a door to the enemy when we avoid certain spiritual mandates. The moment Satan walks through the door we have opened, he locks it behind him, and we are in bondage.

Jesus told—and still tells—His followers that we have a hard time recognizing our own avoidance and neglect:

> *And why worry about a speck in your friend's eye when you have a log in your own? How can you think of saying to your friend, "Let me help you get rid of that speck in your eye," when you can't see past the log in your own eye? Hypocrite! First get rid of the log in your own eye; then you will see well enough to deal with the speck in your friend's eye.*[5]

It is a hard truth that when I am most tempted to criticize someone, it is usually because something substantial is unresolved within *me*. So I fidget with the particle in another person's life and ignore the planet in mine. Lately, if I feel myself shaping a correction to speak, I will stop suddenly and pray, "Lord, why am I reacting to the speck-of-a-fault in that person? What is the plank in me that You want to correct right now? Let's address it quickly before I put a spin on a conversation that I will later regret." Of course, you can guess that after I confront my own issues, I rarely feel qualified to confront anyone else.

Sometimes the key to our release is shaped like a plank. If you allow Jesus to remove what is in you, He will always use it to open the door to your freedom. And what He opens, no one can close.[6]

The change will unlock the chains.

CHAPTER NINE

HE IS TRAINING YOU

*No discipline seems pleasant at the time, but painful.
Later on, however, it produces a harvest of righteousness
and peace for those who have been trained by it.
Therefore, strengthen your feeble arms and weak knees.
"Make level paths for your feet," so that the lame
may not be disabled, but rather healed.*

Hebrews 12:11–12

A FOUR-STAR GENERAL doesn't stoop.

Most of us will never meet this rare senior officer, but we know that, even if he'd never been awarded stripes, titles, and ribbons, the battles this soldier fought or directed were achievements in themselves. A highly decorated military chief may lead with humility and a desire to serve, but a lifetime of sacrifice braces his authority and brings him honor. His experience commands our respect. Everybody knows: You don't become a general by taking it easy. No wonder he stands up straight.

• • •

Several weeks after I survived a brainstem stroke, I saw my battle wounds. I was staying in-patient at a rehabilitation hospital when one of my physical therapists wheeled me past the public restrooms on our usual route. I noticed that there were three bathrooms. By one there was the recognizable black-and-white sign of a woman in a dress. On the other was the black-and-white silhouette of a man in pants. The third sign was blue and white, showing a person in a wheelchair. I had seen those signs thousands of times throughout my life. Now I realized that third sign depicted me.

That's how I look to everyone, I thought. *Seated, not standing. Pushed, not pushing.*

It crossed my mind that I had not seen my reflection since the night I entered the ICU. I had no idea how I looked to others. I decided to wait until everyone left that evening, and then I used a handicapped bar and the rim of the sink to pull myself to an unsteady standing position in front of the mirror in my room.

For the first time, I saw who I had become:

My hair was greasy and parted down the middle, stuck behind my ears.

My eyebrows were thick and bushy; no tweezer had touched them in more than a month.

My lips were peeling and cracked, swollen.

My cheeks were moon-round from steroid treatments in the ICU.

My smile was crooked and foreign to me. The right side of my face drooped slightly.

My face and neck, so sickly pale, were divided by a sharp line: on the left side was a red, bumpy rash, almost a solid deep pink. Later I would learn that this rash was related to my neurological trauma. It followed a perfect line down my stomach and back as well.

My eyes shocked me most. I had felt them jogging in place for days, no longer at rest and controlled. I knew that the head physician at the rehabilitation hospital had asked to document the movement of my eyes with video, so that he could speak about this type of brainstem injury at an upcoming national conference—few patients with my particular neurological trauma had lived to be an example to study. I knew all of this. I knew how sick and dizzy my eyes constantly made me.

It was another thing to *see* them. I fought for breath at the sight. My pupils were dilated; the wide-open whites of my eyes protruded in a seizure of movement. My eyelids were eggshells peeled away from the gripping spasm. I looked permanently startled by Death. Bruised crescents rested heavily in the skin under my eyes.

I stared at myself, a survivor I was meeting for the first time. A stranger's face stared back. A stranger's face, haunted. I was not myself, but a trembling child from a refugee camp. I had barely escaped Death, and I looked like it.

All this time, I had imagined that I appeared the same, just a little tired.

Looking in the mirror that day, I felt I was coming back to the smoking ruins that had once been my home. And for the weeks and months that followed, long after I left the hospital and reenrolled in college—maybe even for years—I was ashamed of my out-of-the-ordinary appearance. People stared at me. Even now I am sometimes self-conscious when I limp into a crowded room, leaning on my cane. I feel people looking, and my posture wilts. Nobody wants the attention of the curious. It is easy to be embarrassed of how we look to others, so avoidance is the path we often take. We want to hide our scarred places, the traces of battles long past, either by not showing up to the party or by not standing up straight when we get there.

But a four-star general doesn't stoop.

Our spiritual lives are described in terms of warfare throughout the Bible. We easily accept the idea that we are in a lifelong battle, but I wonder if the figurative language stops right there, or if there is more for us. What if we extend the metaphor into new and better ways of interpreting our wounds? Perhaps the scars we wish others couldn't see are our service stripes, what's left of our struggle against the enemy. Maybe some scars are evidence of our spiritual experience. We have been through warfare, and coming out with our faith intact is no small thing.

I like to think the enemy quakes when he sees God's wounded warriors taking places of leadership in the church. Our worst life experiences may be *exactly* what qualify us to lead with authority. True discipleship and mentoring is nothing more than guiding one or many believers through combat. Who better for the job than one who bears stripes of his own?

There is a critical verse in Isaiah that I've begun to interpret in a refreshing way. Read Isaiah 53:2–5 with me.

He has no form or comeliness;
And when we see Him,
There is no beauty that we should desire Him.
He is despised and rejected by men,
A Man of sorrows and acquainted with grief.
And we hid, as it were, our faces from Him;
He was despised, and we did not esteem Him.

Surely He has borne our griefs
And carried our sorrows;

Yet we esteemed Him stricken,
Smitten by God, and afflicted.
But He was wounded for our transgressions,
He was bruised for our iniquities;
The chastisement for our peace was upon Him,
And by His stripes *we are healed.* (NKJV)

This is the One who is called the "Commander of the rulers of the earth."[1] There is no one with higher authority than Jesus. In the past, I have understood "His stripes" to mean His wounds. And, yes, that is the original meaning of this text. But what if we view those wounds as military stripes? Does it further cement life-giving truth in our hearts if we think of Jesus as having a spiritual rank that is high above all because of the blows He endured and the battle He won? When He gives an order, the enemy must obey. In His presence, the natural elements stand at attention. Sickness salutes Him. When He says we are healed, we are healed, body and soul. Everything gets into line.

But look closer at something else in this verse. Jesus relied *only* on His authority, not on His appearance. In fact, as Isaiah writes, His wounds were enough to make us hide our faces.

But Jesus kept going anyway.

We are the ones who are tempted not to. Isn't the military veteran with the deeply scarred or deformed face the one who is most tempted to stay out of sight instead of continuing his service in other areas in the community? Maybe he thinks he is repulsive. In the same way, it is the once-broken Christian who is tempted to stay home instead of teaching a Bible study class or reaching out to mentor a new believer. Maybe he thinks he is a failure. Maybe she thinks she is defeated.

After the worst of our winters, we may walk away with scars. Our scars do not define us, but, in a way, they do identify us as survivors. We cannot be more concerned with our appearance than our authority in Christ. We have to look for what is next. The darkest moments of our lives might be the beginning of our divine mission on the earth. So many times, the battlefield is a training ground. We cannot miss the opportunity to put all we have learned to use for the Kingdom. A platoon waits for both the wounded soldier and the repentant Christian. However, if they do not see their scars as service stripes, then they will leave the field and just sit down. I wish they knew that no one is better prepared to stand in spiritual power than the broken and restored among us. The enemy knows they have seen his worst attacks and survived, so the only thing he can do to stop them now is to make them afraid and ashamed of the very thing that brings them honor: faith restored, faith proven true. This is the way Satan wipes out entire armies of Christians. With a lie.

Fear and shame are his weapons of mass deception.

The Lord cries out, "Nooooo! Don't stay quiet! You can't back out of the battle now! I have trained and anointed you! Now you are competent to lead in ways you cannot imagine because My followers will see how your faith has been refined, and they will trust you. Stand up! Feel My strength through your weakness and *stand up*! Lead My people, wounded warrior! Tell them there is nothing to be afraid of anymore! You have survived the warfront and you know better than anyone: with Me, victory is sure!"

Our testimonies are the sacred battle histories of what Christ has done and won. Telling our stories is not a suggestion. In Psalms, it is an order! "Has the LORD redeemed you? Then speak out! Tell others he has redeemed you from your enemies."[2]

In Revelation, Christ Himself calls out to encourage us: You will overcome "by the blood of the Lamb and by the word of [your] testimony!"[3]

Some hear Him calling them into authority, but some never do. They forever fear the appearance of their wounds.

I am convinced that when a church—or a family—appears to be wandering, scattered, and lost, it is because somewhere a soldier sees his scars as his shame instead of his stripes. He doesn't know he has been trained.

So he leaves the platoon that the Lord meant for him to lead.

CHAPTER TEN

HE WILL REWARD YOU

And I will give you treasures hidden in the darkness—
secret riches. I will do this so you may know that
I am the LORD, the God of Israel,
the one who calls you by name.

Isaiah 45:3 NLT

MY THREE-YEAR-OLD NEPHEW and his sisters were playing with Pla-Doh in the kitchen while their parents were in the living room. Suddenly it became quiet. A little too quiet.

"Hey, what are y'all doing in there?" my sister-in-law called out.

"Anythiiiing . . . ," he answered, using the same tone an older child would have used to say he was doing *nothing*. That is what he had meant, that he was doing nothing important. Needless to say, my sister-in-law took that as her cue to sprint into the kitchen.

My nephew didn't realize it, but he had perfectly captured a profound idea. When we are doing nothing, we truly *are* doing anything. And vice versa. When we begin any day without a to-do list or a calendar or at least some plan . . . we end up doing anything at all, which adds up to nothing important by nightfall.

We have to be intentional in order to do something.

Maybe intentionality is the core message of one of the verses that has always been a mystery to me.

James 1:2–4 tells us to do something that feels impossible: "Consider it *pure joy*, my brothers and sisters, whenever you face trials of many kinds, because you know that the testing of your faith produces perseverance. Let perseverance finish its work so that you may be mature and complete, not lacking anything."

Pure joy? When we read that we are to think of trials as pure joy, we are flabbergasted.

One of my friends has lost her only sibling and she has had eighteen major surgeries herself—from digestive surgery to brain surgery—in the span of five years. And she almost lost her own life during the births of both of her children. Some of you would agree with her that trials in and of themselves don't feel much like joy.

Ah, but James is not telling us that trials should *feel* like joy. He is telling us that we are to *think* of them as joy, which means that there is mental work to be done. And that work is best described in terms of a heart transplant.

Follow me. The word *courage* enters the English language from a French word that means *heart*. In fact, when we see a bold and courageous person, we often say, "He has heart." Courage is the heart of us. As long as courage keeps rhythm inside our chests, we are awake and alive. But without it, we can't go on. When our courage gives out, therefore, we need a transplant from someone who feels stronger and more filled with faith. The heart transplant process is called *encouragement*. Encouragement is the act of transplanting heart from one person into another, from transplanting courage from one person into another. Encouragers can deliberately place courage *in* us.

Joy is a little different from courage. Joy is like blood. As long as it runs through our days, we live full and healthy lives. Without it, we wither slowly. Thankfully, there is a solution for diminishing joy: a transfusion. When we cannot find joy easily, we can make a decision to transfer joy straight from the Holy Spirit into our circumstances. The transfusion process is called *enjoyment*. *En*joyment is the act of infusing joy into a situation. Joy is the fruit of the Spirit, so we have to ask God for it. The Holy Spirit can deliberately place joy *in* our trials.

These medical analogies are not too far-fetched. "A cheerful heart is good like medicine," the Bible tells us.[1]

The New Living Translation offers a few different words to express James 1:2–4, and they make the mystery much clearer. The translators interpret James's writing this way: "Dear brothers and sisters, when troubles come your way, consider it an *opportunity for great joy*. For you know that when your faith is tested, your endurance has a chance to grow. So let it grow, for when your endurance is fully developed, you will be perfect and complete, needing nothing."

Trials are not a great joy in and of themselves. But they are an *opportunity* for great joy. That's different.

• • •

Earlier this year, I started thinking of inconveniences as spiritual workouts. When one of my students would have a behavioral meltdown in the classroom, I would stop before I disciplined from annoyance instead of from love and whisper to myself, "This is just an exercise." Or when a family member would do something that really irritated or hurt me, I would stop before replying rudely and breathe in, "This is just an exercise." Or when I would go to my post office box day after day for six weeks, and the check I desperately needed still hadn't come, I would grit my teeth day after day, close the box day after day, and mutter day after day, "This is just an exercise." Or when the mayonnaise in the blender exploded all over my shirt, or when I tripped and fell in the grocery store, or when I had a fender bender *with a parked car*, I would say with all of my soul's resolve, "This is . . . *just* . . . an exercise."

Thinking of life's simple difficulties as exercises—or as opportunities to increase our inner strength—somehow makes them a little easier to handle for me. These daily exercises prepare us for more difficult things. Our plan should be to "max out" on faith as a response to a major calamity when it comes. A tragedy can't be our very first work out. We won't be able to handle it unless we have done the smaller daily workouts in advance. When we regularly, purposefully try to lift the heavy weights of patience and forgiveness in each situation, *that* is learning to apply faith, and it is spiritual exercise. Then when a catastrophe hits, the outcome is much better than if we had had no weight-lifting experience at all. We will find ourselves acting with more control and kindness. We will discover nights of real rest in the Lord. We will not fall into deep wells of fear.

If we can be intentional about applying faith to difficulty, then we can be intentional about adding joy to difficulty as well. *Applying faith* must be on our to-do list. *Adding joy* has to be part of the plan. If we are not intentional about both, we will end up doing anything *but* being faithful and joyful.

Anything.

Only in the sense that we are intentional in expecting the Holy Spirit to put joy *into* our trials do we *en*joy them. I cannot explain how to go about adding joy or how the transfusion of enjoyment occurs, but miraculously, it does. I think of the verse in Isaiah 45:3 (NLT) where God promises to give us the "treasures hidden in the darkness—secret riches." Though God is addressing a specific historical situation in that context, we can certainly apply that verse to ourselves. He always gives us precious rewards—even joy—during periods of cold and dark suffering, if we will but look for them.

I discovered this in the midst of a period of distress in my life. A series of events seemed to be leading to a failure that would be impossible for anyone to reverse. I felt afraid. I didn't know what to do, I had no one to lean on. Finally, after a month of worry, I turned on a praise playlist, sat down on the floor, and wept, "That's it! I give up! I will just praise until I find some kind of treasure in this darkness. You have never failed before, and You won't start now."

I sang for more than an hour, and by the end of the playlist, tears streamed down my face. At first, I had felt no real emotion over the words of the songs, but eventually my heart warmed into a peaceful awareness of His presence. I was totally confident in Him and totally free and felt totally loved. My worries suddenly seemed like gnats, not monsters.

And *there* was my reward.

"It's You!" I prayed. "It's YOU! *You* are the treasure in darkness, Lord."

There is no other form of reward that compares to the glory of more of Him.

The Holy Spirit is deep and full enough to share all of Himself with everyone who is willing to ask. Asking is not hard work. Humbling ourselves to ask *is*. If you have a problem finding treasure, your real problem may be pride. That is the way it has always been with me. The more stubborn I am, wanting things to turn out the way I want, the more miserable I am. The more I let go and submit to God's unfolding plan, the more content I am.

Paul writes to the church in Philippi, "I know what it is to be in need, and I know what it is to have plenty. I have learned the secret of being *content* in any and every situation, whether well fed or hungry, whether living in plenty or in want."

What is the secret, Paul?

"I can do all this *through him* who gives me strength" (Philippians 4:12–13).

Just God. That's the secret.

In the natural winter, a great, big coat makes the

difference between misery and coziness. In the winter of the soul, the nearness of God makes the same difference. He is the secret that makes suffering bearable.

What about the optimists? They always seem joyful. They wear smiles and make positive comments, and we wonder if they are being fake or if they are clueless. It is hard to believe that they are real. But look closely, or you will miss the evidence of their search. They have been mining in the dark cave of the situation they never wanted, in order to find a thin, gold vein of contentment in the rock. Reaching it is one of their rewards. All we see is their sparkle and shine. We don't know the gritty work they have done in order to find the treasure of joy.

God will give you something of great value in the darkness. Sometimes the treasures He gives us are tender moments or sweet gestures from others. Sometimes they come in the form of provision or a complete change in circumstance. But always, always, always, our reward is a greater awareness of His nearness. It might take some exercise. It might take some work. Heaven forbid we become so harried that we leave this truth buried. If we dig for hidden treasure on our journey instead of just walking past it, then it will be ours. We will know without doubting that He is close to us. We will know that He is near and all we need.

And that *is* pure joy.

CHAPTER ELEVEN

HE WILL NOT LEAVE YOU

Where can I go from your Spirit?
Where can I flee from your presence?
If I go up to the heavens, you are there;
if I make my bed in the depths, you are there.
If I rise on the wings of the dawn,
if I settle on the far side of the sea,
even there your hand will guide me,
your right hand will hold me fast.

Psalm 139:7–10

I PANICKED WHEN I couldn't find the notes pages that I had been working on for months. The steering committee from this women's conference had asked me to speak a year in advance, and for a long time I had been praying and studying in preparation for the opportunity. They had needed my presentation title six months early in order to print the programs, and because I had based the teaching on a passage from the Sermon on the Mount, I told them the title would be "What to Do When You Fall, Little Sparrow." I had filled pages and pages with my thoughts, but then suddenly lost them all the week before the conference, when I would normally be finalizing the message.

I shuffled through papers on every counter and flat surface. My house turned into a mess as I looked. The more I searched, the worse it became. I was frazzled and decided that I just needed to reboot. Breathing slowly, I tried to think of something that would relax me enough to start looking again with a clear mind and clear eyes. Suddenly swimming seemed to be just the thing that would bring refreshment. I had to make myself calm down, and in a pool I would be forced to stop looking and just swim or float.

I got ready, drove to the indoor pool at the city's recreation center, and headed inside the big, double glass doors. A man held open the first set of doors, and I thanked him as I stepped into the entryway. As I made my way toward the second set of doors, I tripped. Sprawling to the side, I slammed against the picture window, hitting my hip and my elbow on the aluminum framework near the floor. I lay there on my back and did not move.

"Do you need help? Do you need help?!" A facilities manager and a personal trainer came running when they saw me fall. The gentleman who had been holding the door leaned over to try to pull my arm. Sitting up, I waved all of them off. It is so hard for me to speak when I am in physical pain. I can't explain how it feels to lose all words. It is a residual neurological effect from my stroke. If I try to speak, my mouth will not correctly form sounds, and it is challenging to understand what I am saying. Sometimes it is hard for me to breathe. It is easier to sit still and wait for the subsiding waves of pain to pass. Then I can speak clearly without slurring my speech too badly.

The people who were trying to help me would not back off. Other people were entering the gym by way of the other door as I sat there in the entryway. I just needed a few minutes to myself. I could not have moved up into the chair that they had brought over for me.

"Get up. Get up, ma'am. Can you get up?" they kept asking.

"I know her; let me talk to her." Randi, a lifelong friend of mine, ran over and eased into the small group. She had been on a treadmill when she saw me fall. She realized that I wasn't talking to anyone and leaned over and whispered close to my face, "You okay?"

I nodded.

"Can you get up?"

I shook my head.

"Is it hard to talk?"

I nodded.

"Okay, then let's just sit here a minute," she said to me. Then turning to the people around us, she said, "Y'all, why don't we just give her a minute. I think she is going to be all right. She just needs awhile to collect her thoughts."

"Can you help us get her into this chair?" the facilities manager asked.

"No, thank you very much. She would feel better just staying where she is for a minute. I'll stay with her. We'll be all right. You don't have to wait here with us."

It took some talking, but finally everyone left. Then Randi gave me one of the sweetest gifts any friend can give: presence.

"There," she said when they were gone. She sat down on the floor beside me, crossing her legs. "Let's just be still and quiet a little while."

For ten minutes neither one of us said a word. She didn't touch me. She didn't ask me questions. She didn't look at her phone at all, and that one impressed me the most. She was *fully* present with me in that moment. We both sat, looking out the glass doors in silence.

She just stayed beside me. She was not going to leave me.

I inhaled. Finally, I was ready to talk. "I'm okay. I think I can stand up now."

"Okay, good," she said, "But before you try, I want you

to make a plan for what we are going to do after you stand up, because your elbow needs to be seen by a doctor."

"No, it doesn't," I said. "It hurts, but not that bad. It is not broken or anything. See? I can move it." I bent my elbow and tried to look around my forearm at it. Then I straightened it and tried to look over my shoulder at it.

"You cannot see your elbow from the angle I can see it. Trust what I am saying. You are going to need stitches."

I tried to argue with her one more time before she convinced me to look at my reflection in the window.

Oh. I *did* need stitches.

By the time I got home from the urgent care center with five new stitches that afternoon, I was exhausted. *Oh, yeah! And I still need to do something about my lost notes*, I remembered, sitting down in the nearest chair. I didn't have the energy to look for them anymore, so I grabbed a pencil, paper, and clipboard and started trying to re-create what I had written. Keeping my wounded elbow off the armrest, I wrote the title on the top of the paper.

"What to Do When You Fall, Little Sparrow."

It hadn't occurred to me until *that moment* that I had fallen during the search for my notes about falling. Tears filled my eyes. My original notes had been about God's provision and about the sweet knowledge that He knows us and our needs even before we ask Him. I had taken the title from the Sermon on the Mount, when Jesus says He is aware of everything. He is even aware when a sparrow falls, so how much more is He aware when *we* fall?

It was obvious that the timing of the title and the loss of notes and the fall in the recreation center had worked together for my good. God was pointing me to something new. With my elbow throbbing, I ditched the idea of rewriting my old notes and started to write fresh ones.

"What is this lesson *really* about, Lord?"

And I wrote.

• • •

This is what to do when you fall, little sparrow:

First, you don't have to get up right away. When you experience a devastating loss or a period of trauma, people are going to want you to get up pretty quickly. Sometimes I think this is because they want to be able to move on themselves. People mean well. They want what is best for you, so love them for loving you. But you may have to hint that everybody's timetable is different. There are some people, like me, who may have to take awhile to gather their thoughts, and that's okay. After you fall, you do not have to get up until it is time.

The second thing you need to remember is that you don't have to talk until you are ready. Again, people are going to want, even *need*, you to start talking. This is basic triage, right? After an accident, we make sure people can breathe by asking them to talk. But in real life, you might not feel ready to talk after a heart blow. Don't hold your breath too long, but don't begin before you're ready, either. When you are not talking to other people, it doesn't mean that you are not talking at all. You are probably talking a lot. To yourself and to God, which is important. Talking to a friend is critical too, so talk. But talk when you are ready.

Third, be aware that you need a friend who can see what you can't. Not every wound is perceptible to you. Sometimes it takes looking from another angle. From an angle *outside* the situation. This is why it is vital to pick good friends, because later, they will have a significant job to do. They are the ones who know you well enough to know when you are really hurt and in need of help, even when you don't want to admit it. Investing time and effort to find an experienced, Bible-based counselor can be just the help you need; they can enrich your life and ensure that your wound heals cleanly. We cannot overlook the importance of the community God has provided.

Friends, family, mentors, and counselors will never be able to say and do all of the things we think we need them to, but, on the other hand, they can say and do so much *more* than we think we need them to. The colder it is in winter, the more we need to huddle together for warmth.

God is the perfect Friend. He is the Friend who sits beside you until you are ready to take His hand and get up. He is the Friend who waits patiently until you are ready to talk to Him again. He is the Friend who can see so deeply into your heart, and He knows the areas you need healing, even when you don't.

A key component in healing is time. There is often a period of time after serious distress that we might not feel very much like being in God's presence. We may have been broken to the point that we can't understand anything about Him anymore.

During those times, this precious promise is what we need: "What if some did not have faith? Will their lack of faith nullify God's faithfulness? Not at all!"[1]

And this: "If we are faithless, he will remain faithful, for he cannot disown himself."[2]

Sometimes hope hunters have to sit down awhile and catch their breath.

God is not going to leave you. He will be there when you are ready to get up. He will be there when you are ready to talk. He will be there when you are ready to dress your wound.

He will not leave you. You can take the time you need.

CHAPTER TWELVE

HE WILL NOT FORGET YOU

*God is not unjust; he will not forget your work
and the love you have shown him as you
have helped his people and continue to help them.*

Hebrews 6:10

WE REMEMBER the stories of our scars:

The Houston sun was full and hot. I stood, poised on my friend's bike, as a neighborhood boy slowly backed his rear tire up to my rear tire. A drop of sweat slung from the tip of my nose as I turned around to look at him. He glared at me.

"You ready?"

I had made a bigmouthed bet that a girl could beat a boy in a bike race any day. The plan was to head in opposite directions around the block and to meet up, bike to bike, in the same place. One problem with that plan was that I was motivated only by hardheaded determination.

I wanted to prove myself capable as the lone girl who had interjected herself into a previously all-boy race. Another problem with the plan was that my competitor lived in that neighborhood, and I didn't. He was a friend of the friend whose bike I was borrowing. He knew the block we would be racing because it was *his* block. I, on the other hand, lived five hours away; I was just visiting on our summer vacation.

We jumped forward when my friend yelled, "Go!" And I only raced a few feet before I ran into something in the road. I landed, face-first, on the pavement.

I remember every tiny detail about that trip to the emergency room: sights, smells, and sounds. For a couple weeks I had five stitches under a thick bandage on my chin. To this day, the scent of hydrogen peroxide can take me back to fifth grade, without fail. I still have the scar.

The moral of that story is: If it begins with a bet, it probably ends with regret.

• • •

There was also the time when I was taking a color photography course in college, and I was hurrying to finish a major project. The hallway was poorly organized. On my way back into the darkroom, my foot struck a rolled-up carpet that was lying next to the wall, and I fell forward, throwing my photo-developing supplies to the ceiling. I reached out both hands to break my fall, and my palms pushed open a door—which had been almost all the way open, but not quite. My knees hit the tiles, and my hands squeaked down the door to the floor. I slowly leaned back to sit on my ankles. My knees were hurting. But it wasn't over. The mousetrap was still moving. Above my head, wrapped around the doorknob of that door, was an electrical cord. The cord had pulled taut when the door had slammed wide. Right next to where I was kneeling and trying to catch my breath, a waist-high bookcase stood against the hallway wall. On top of it was an out-of-order, fifty-plus-pound enlarger. An enlarger looks like an enormous metal microscope, with sharp angles everywhere.

You guessed it. The cord that was wrapped around the doorknob that was on the door that I had opened when I fell because my foot struck an old carpet . . . was attached to the enlarger. A corner of it gouged my head on its way down. It landed on my back.

I remember everything that happened next, all the students and the professor who came running to pull the enlarger off of me and roll me upright. In dazed pain, I couldn't speak. So I did what *anyone* would do. I started communicating in sign language, of course. I actually sat there, leaning against the wall, with blood running down my face and my fingers flying madly. Keep two things in mind as you imagine this stupid scene. Number one: I don't actually *know* sign language. I took one semester of ASL in college, but for all intents and purposes, I still only know the letters and numbers that I memorized from the *Encyclopedia Britannica* when I was eleven. Number two: there wasn't anyone who knew sign language in that class. Not even the alphabet.

Then one girl saw my frantic signs and yelled, "Oh! She's *deaf*." Yes, she thought I was deaf. It was the end of the semester, we'd been working around each other three times a week for sixteen weeks, I had never shown any other indication that I could not hear, but suddenly she thought I was deaf. I guess I had kept a low profile in class, I don't know. Anyway, they ran to get a girl she knew who was in a class on the same hall. That girl ran to us, knelt in front of me, and started signing. Which, of course, I could not understand because—*ahem*—I do not know sign language. But my mouth still wasn't working, so I tried to spell it out for her. I-D-O-N-O-T-K-N-O-W-A-N-Y-R-E-A-L-S-I-G-N-L-A-N-G-U-A-G-E-W-O-R-D-S-I-J-U-S-T-K-N-O-W-T-H-E-L-E-T-T-E-R-S-A-N-D-N-U-M-B-E-R-S! So we sat there, fingering nonsense to one another, and no one ever went to get a piece of paper and a pencil. I know there were some around, too, because we were on a college campus, for goodness' sake. But apparently the people who go to college, *need* to be in college, because no one actually thought of a paper and pencil.

I ended up with three stitches on the top of my head, and my skull has a dime-sized dent there, which I am going to call worth it, because now I have a ridiculous story to tell for the rest of my life.

And the moral of that story is: There are ways to make something stupid even stupider.

●   ●   ●

And there was the time when I slammed my finger in the car door. And it locked. And the keys were inside my purse. And the purse was hanging on the shoulder of the arm that had the hand that had the finger that was locked in the car door. I danced a dance of pain for five minutes, trying to set myself free with only my left hand. Try to unlock your car with the hand you don't usually use. Just try it. I almost dropped my keys sixty times.

When I finally opened the door, I saw that my middle finger needed stitches. As you know by now, I am some-what useless when I am in pain. Oh, the fun of a nervous system after a brainstem injury.

I knew I couldn't drive myself to the ER. I ran to bang my good fist on the door of my neighbor/landlord, the guy who lived in the other side of the duplex. I always just slid the rent check through the mail slot in his door. I didn't really know him, but I'd talked with him a couple times. Once about the plumbing and once when I agreed to feed his dog while he was out of town. He seemed nice enough, so I decided to ask him for help. When he answered the door, bleary-eyed and in a stupor in the middle of the day, I should have known something was wrong. Still, I begged him to take me to the hospital.

He helped me into the passenger seat of his truck and tried to buckle me in like a little baby in a carseat.

"Forget it! No seat belt!" I yelled, holding my bloody hand above my head. "Just drive! Let's get there as fast as we can!" As he walked around the car to get behind the wheel, I prayed, "Dear Lord, please save the end of my finger! Dear Lord, please save my finger!"

It wasn't until he got in and closed the driver-side door that I smelled the alcohol.

Then I realized for the first time that I was in the car with a total stranger who was drunk, I was not wearing a seatbelt, and I had just told him to speed. Immediately, I prayed inwardly, "Dear Lord! Forget about my finger! Forget the finger! Just save *my life*!"

Three stitches left a scar that still makes me smile.

And the moral of that story is: Prayer is all about priorities.

· · ·

If we had time, and you were ready to laugh, I could tell you the ludicrous stories of every scar I have. I remember the details brilliantly. I bet you could tell me yours too. Our ordinary days, we cannot remember. But the days that marked us for life? Those we cannot forget.

Scars are vivid reminders.

· · ·

There are times I have felt forsaken and forgotten by God. I know you have too. I know you have felt this because even Jesus felt it.

"My God, my God, why have you forsaken me?" He cried on the cross. Jesus knew He had not been forsaken by God, but it felt that way.

When this is recorded in Matthew 27:46, Jesus is actually quoting Psalm 22, a poem that David wrote. If Jesus, the only Divine, felt forsaken, and if David, the greatest warrior in history, felt forsaken, then we know the feeling must be universal.

We all have felt forgotten. Forsakenness feels like lost

hope. When we cannot see hope, we might feel forgotten most of all.

Maybe that is why God tells us so many times in the Bible that He has not forsaken us or forgotten us. My favorite incidence of one of these reminders is in Isaiah 49:15–16:

> *Can a mother forget the baby at her breast*
> *   and have no compassion on the child she has borne?*
> *Though she may forget,*
> *   I will not forget you!*
> *See, I have engraved you on the palms of my hands;*
> *   your walls are ever before me.*

We are engraved. We are His scars.

The problem is not that *He* forgets how much He loves us; the problem is that *we* forget how much He loves us. Of course He remembers us. How could He forget the story of His wounds? And all this time we have been singing to children that "He's got the whole world in His hands" when that isn't exactly true.

He has the whole world *on* His hands.

And He remembers.

CHAPTER THIRTEEN

HE WILL CARRY YOU

Shout for joy, you heavens; rejoice,
you earth; burst into song, you mountains!
For the LORD comforts his people
and will have compassion on his afflicted ones.

Isaiah 49:13

I OPENED THE OVERSIZED envelope with curiosity. I couldn't think of anyone who was planning a wedding, so I was eager to see whose name would be on the invitation. My fingers found the RSVP card first. I looked at it twice, opening my eyes wider the longer I looked. The blanks had already been filled out in blue ballpoint pen.

Number of guests attending: 1

This was just to save me any confusion, I guess. They were letting me know I didn't have a choice. I was expected to come without a guest.

• • •

After deciding that I didn't need to be attending a Sunday-morning Bible class with "college-aged singles" or even with "young professionals" anymore, I started seeking a class in which I could really study the Word and grow . . . unclassified by age or marital status. But most church classes still are separated by rudimentary life-station descriptors. Sometimes it feels like I am back registering for classes in undergrad, and marriage or kids are the prerequisites to taking a course. One day, I disregarded that and went into a "young marrieds" class anyway, because that's where most of my friends were. When class was about to start, the facilitator said to me, "What are you doing in the young marrieds class, Nika? Come back when you have a ring on your finger." I was so angry, I swallowed hot tears for thirty-five minutes until class was over, and then I never went back.

• • •

A few years later, I tried again, in a different church. I looked at the class list at the information desk, and there was nothing except various family-themed classes and a generic class for "college-aged singles." Exploring the hallway, I walked up to one classroom door and stared at the sign for five minutes: *Sermon on the Mount for Young Families*. I couldn't make myself walk in, yet I couldn't make myself walk away. I kept thinking, *Why is this class for young families? Isn't the Sermon on the Mount for everyone?* I went to the church coffee shop to wait for an hour until the main assembly began.

• • •

After a Bible study one night, someone came over and asked me to be praying for her daughter. "Please pray for her. It is so sad. She turns twenty-seven next month, and she is not married yet."

It's so sad?

At the time she said it, I was one week from my fortieth birthday. If being unmarried at twenty-seven is sad, what is it called to be unmarried at thirty-nine? I didn't want to pray for this friend. I wanted to punch her. But I took her hands in mine and prayed sincerely for her daughter anyway. Also, I was praying that God would give me patience not to speak my mind. It wasn't the time.

• • •

Eventually, I hit a wall.

Most of the time I joyfully jog through each day, knowing deep in my soul that God has a plan and perfect timing for me, knowing that I am right where He wants me. Sure, there are things I have always desired for myself, but I hold loosely to my goals for my life, trusting the Lord to lead me toward even better goals. I've had so many amazing experiences that I would not have known if I had been married in my twenties. But when I was looking down forty's throat and was still without a family of my own—something I have always wanted—I suddenly felt sick about it. Even the church no longer felt like home. I couldn't connect there like I used to, which I knew was dangerous. I felt a stormfront closing in on my heart. There is warmth in community, but when I looked, I didn't see any room for me around the campfire. I started to resent not being married, but it wasn't just about being single.

What I *really* resented was not being where I thought I would be. I had always imagined my life would look a certain way by the time I reached this moment and place. Everything is different than I had anticipated. Sometimes that realization is all it takes to usher in the winter:

I never thought it would be like this.

Disappointment fell on my shoulders like a lead apron in an X-ray room, which is an appropriate analogy, because everywhere I went, I felt like everyone could see right through me. I felt exposed and vulnerable. The enemy aimed at his target. Then he launched a machine-gun spray of rude comments in my direction:

"A pretty girl like you . . . why aren't you married?"

"You won't understand until you have kids."

"Must be nice using your whole paycheck on only one person."

"Don't you ever date? We gotta work on getting you someone."

If they weren't picking on me, they were trying to fix me. This made it difficult to cultivate contentment, which is what God was urging me to do. Through one zinger after another, I focused on my lack instead of on my task.

For years I have known that I am called by God to share biblical truth through writing and speaking, and I became worried when I sensed that a lot of people did not have respect for my teaching because I did not have experience with marriage and parenthood. I lost my grip on God's affirming words to me and started paying attention to everyone else's words. Every day my mind rehearsed the same skewed version of my story: *I've been disregarded. I've been overlooked. I have no place in the church. Will I ever have a meaningful ministry if people think I am not qualified? Do my life experiences mean nothing?*

Worry turned into fury, but my anger was just a flimsy self-protection. Anger gave way to ache. The ache, the crushing ache, that followed anger is hard for me to describe. For five months, I cried. I felt useless. Devoid of influence. Insignificant to the church at large.

And here I am, still deeply desiring a child of my own, while my friends are already having their third or fourth child. Many of my friends' children already are starting high school, and it stings because I had always hoped our children would grow up together. Most of their growing is already done. When the lead apron fell on me, I felt like I had waited long enough for a family. That was it. I couldn't bring myself to look at my friends' pictures on social media anymore. It hurt too much. I stopped being able to rejoice with those who rejoice.

"Just adopt a child," a friend said flippantly. As if anyone who adopts a child *just adopts* a child.

Then I really thought about it. I started researching how to adopt a child as a single person, but someone who has systemic lupus erythematosis and a history of stroke can't get health insurance, much less a child. Adoption was a dead-end idea that lasted only a minute.

I didn't want to let anyone in on my pain. I felt embarrassed to be feeling so awful for what seemed like an illegitimate reason. People talk as if the ache of infertility only applies to people who are married. They don't even consider that it also would affect the unmarried Christian who has chosen to reserve intimacy for marriage. Finally, I decided to be honest and open up to a few friends, so that I would not stay in isolation. Their responses were not always as empathetic as I had hoped.

I know they meant well. People don't know what to say about the deep desire for a child, whether it is the result of chastity before marriage or the result of a medical condition after marriage. People don't know what to say or do about pain in general.

Even me. After my own lengthy hospital stays, I *swore* that I would say and do all the right things the next time one of my friends was in the hospital. I was going to be The Most Supportive Friend in the World. I thought I had learned from the wonderful ways I had been treated and from the thoughtless ways I had been treated while in the hospital, so now I would know exactly what to do.

Except I didn't.

The next time a friend was in the hospital, I planned a huge gift basket, but then I procrastinated too long. So I planned a simple visit, but then I couldn't think of a good time to go. So I planned a phone call, but then I couldn't think of what to say about having taken so long. So I planned a get-well card, but I couldn't find the perfect one. So I planned an e-mail, but that felt like a complete joke. So I didn't do anything.

People are rarely, if ever, going to say and do the right

things, even if they promise themselves they will. Humans have too much human in them.

I didn't think I knew anyone who would understand this vaporous ache, so I have quit saying anything to anyone. People tend to think an unmarried person is lonely, but that is not it. I am not lonely, but I *am* looking forward to sharing life and pursuing God with my husband. Until then, I am tired of *one* aspect of my life keeping me from *many* things I want. And I am tired of taking care of everything—from where I buy a house to where I buy car insurance—all by myself. All of the decisions, all of the work, all of the responsibility is mine.

Jesus is always beside me, but He doesn't take the trash to the curb. He doesn't help me clean the pool. Instead, He gives me the patience, gives me the inner strength, gives me the grace, and gives me the wisdom to do it myself.

But that doesn't mean it isn't hard sometimes. For five dark months, I cried so hard my stomach hurt, and often my cries turned into prayer. I wasn't begging for my circumstances to change. I was begging for increased strength to bear the heaviness until it lifted again. I truly believe in feeling deeply, instead of hurrying ourselves out of pain. So I kept asking God, "What are You teaching me during this darkness, Lord?" I wrote in my journal a lot. At times, I physically couldn't breathe under the weight of sorrow, and I had to believe there was a reason for that. I sensed that I was learning important lessons about seeking the Lord during yet another distinct season of darkness, so that I could share hope with other people. *Winter will bring spring in me; winter will bring spring in me*, I repeated. Week after week, month after month, I poured out my heart before the Lord. And on one rare and lovely night, He answered.

This is grief, He said.

Through tears, I argued, "No, no, it is not grief. I haven't lost anything. There has to be a different name for hurting over something I have never had."

It is grief.

"Well, yes, I'm mourning. I am mourning the absence of children I have never met, longing to speak names I do not know, wanting to hold hands I've never touched."

For the next few minutes, I thought of my recent pain as an expression of grief, and I sobbed. Yes, when you long for a family and do not have one, it can feel like an uncategorized loss. No one will ever send you a card in your bereavement or bring you a casserole. No one will ever ask how you are getting along, and you don't want them to. It is a solitary and marginalized grief. It is an ache no one acknowledges.

"Okay, Lord, I can see it is grief, but it is such a small

grief. I have a friend who lost her husband, and that is a big grief. That is a huge weight. I am only carrying small things: I'm longing for a family, I have a chronic illness, I have a disability . . . Each of these burdens is heavy but not impossible."

Two-thousand pounds is two-thousand pounds, He said.

Suddenly I saw a scene clearly in my mind. It was a remarkable memory from my youth. While I was growing up, my family had one special possession: an antique piano. This ornate piano, built in 1898, weighed half a ton. Over the years we moved homes many times, and each time the movers would groan upon seeing the piano. More than one set of movers refused to touch it at all. One particular move stood apart from the others. When we got to that house, my mother led the movers toward the singular entryway that could be used to bring the piano into the house. There was a small flight of stairs leading to the door. It was the only way in.

Two burly men carried that heavy piano up a flight of stairs, step after difficult step.

Two men may be carrying a piano up a staircase, but only *one* of them truly bears the weight. Halfway up, the man on the bottom started to struggle. My mother felt so badly seeing the men strain. But there was no other way in, and it was impossible for the men to step back down.

The man on the bottom set his jaw, took one more step, and then the blood vessels in his nose burst. The pressure had become too much. Blood ran down over his mouth, and he couldn't even take his hand off of the piano to wipe it away.

In my heart, I saw myself in that picture, carrying an ache of great weight. I couldn't even let go of it long enough to wipe the blood from my nose. There was no way to put the heaviness down.

Again the Lord spoke, *Two-thousand pounds is two-thousand pounds, whether you are carrying one circumstance or many small circumstances.*

The weight of many things was too much. He was letting me know that He could see that I was bursting as I carried it all. That night, I cried myself to sleep again.

Nothing miraculous happened the next day. My situation didn't change, not in any area. But something inside me did. In the morning, I felt that some of the burden had lifted. Somehow, just knowing that God could see me, that He knew the heaviness of what was in my arms, made it easier to move upward and onward. Some time later, I noticed that it had been days since I had grieved. God's presence had filled my life as I purposefully returned to the Word.

Months later, when I thought back to that slow

transformation from sorrow to joy, I could only trace it to the night He showed me the piano movers. Through that image, God had comforted me. It meant a great deal to know that He knows how weighty life can be. I felt I was becoming stronger in His presence, but I still held some of the ache.

Real relief had yet to come. In my life, God loves the slow reveal.

Remembering the vision of the piano movers one night, I prayed, "Thank You so much for helping me move the heavy stuff, God. We're in this together. As long as I have to be the man on the bottom, it is comforting to know that You've got it from the top."

Gently He whispered, *Nika, I am the man on the bottom.*

That's when I knew He wasn't just carrying my burden. He was carrying *me*.

CHAPTER FOURTEEN

HE WILL SPEAK TO YOU

I lie in the dust; revive me by your word.
I told you my plans, and you answered.
Now teach me your decrees.
Help me understand the meaning
of your commandments, and I will meditate
on your wonderful deeds.
I weep with sorrow; encourage me by your word.
Keep me from lying to myself;
give me the privilege of knowing your instructions.
I have chosen to be faithful;
I have determined to live by your regulations.

Psalm 119:25–30 NLT

NOT MANY PEOPLE are crazy enough to volunteer to be a senior class sponsor. If you see me signing up for it again, please knock the pen out of my hand. The year that I took on that role, I learned one critical truth: I didn't thank my own high school teachers enough. It is an unbelievable stress to help six hundred seniors navigate what they firmly believe are the most important nine months of their lives.

Part of my responsibility during my brief stint in this high-pressure position was guiding the class officers through weeks and weeks of planning the prom. That year we held it at the Texas Motor Speedway, in a ballroom high above the NASCAR racetrack. When the important night rolled around, it was worth every effort spent in preparation, partly because the venue felt like a fairy tale. The night sky sparkling through the floor-to-ceiling windows was the perfect backdrop for a memorable evening.

But those windows were almost the perfect backdrop for a weather catastrophe too. The evening that began like a dream almost ended like a nightmare.

Not long after the waitstaff cleared the dinner tables, the dancing began. It didn't last long. The manager found me and let me know that there was a tornado warning in the area. We would have to evacuate the ballroom immediately. The music stopped, and the other senior sponsor stood on the stage, explaining the situation over a microphone. We asked everyone to begin moving to the hallways, where they would need to crouch on the floor until the emergency passed. But students who had invested months of thought, time, money, and energy into the special night were not quick to give it up. There wasn't a girl in the place who was eager to sit on the floor in her sequined gown.

The students didn't seem to be paying attention. The girls leisurely turned to their dates, asking them to retrieve purses and other items from the tables. Some stopped to take one more sip of ice water.

"Hurry!" I said, ushering them off the dance floor. "This is an urgent situation. Walk quickly! We have to get a safe distance away from these windows! Now!"

The ballroom lights came on, squelching the atmosphere. Still, the students walked slowly. The boys carefully escorted their dates through the maze of decorated tables. Every one of them was keeping his cool.

"Listen! Let's move *out*!" I yelled over the rising wind outside.

They meandered.

Then there was a sound that was louder than my voice. The sky through the windows turned white. A crack of thunder near the racetrack shook the water glasses and made us jump. The imminence of the storm changed everything. At the sound of it, everyone listened. You should have seen those girls hike up their skirts and run in their heels, the boys following closely behind.

This, of course, is analogous to how we behave sometimes. God wants us to pay attention to Him. He speaks every day, but we are not motivated to listen closely to the Word when the skies are clear. It is usually only when there is an approaching catastrophe that we pay attention and take action.

But we don't have to wait for the thunder.

• • •

You would think it would be easy for someone to pay attention and listen if an angel walked into the room. But it seems that some people in the Bible who received angelic visitations weren't hearing very well.

In Judges 6, the Israelites are starving and under terrible oppression from Midian, so God sends a heavenly messenger to an average guy named Gideon. He is a farmer. He has never been in a battle of any kind, but the angel greets him by saying, "The Lord is with you, *mighty warrior*."

Obviously, God is not hesitant in bestowing affirmation upon His servants. Gideon doesn't have to ask the Lord for a vote of confidence; all he has to do is pay attention to the one he just heard.

Daniel receives a similar salutation in Daniel 10:11 when a celestial being appears to him in order to interpret a bizarre vision he'd had.

The angel says, "Daniel, *you who are highly esteemed*,

consider carefully the words I am about to speak to you, and stand up, for I have now been sent to you."

Again, the Lord is quick to affirm Daniel if he is ready to hear it.

He does this for Mary too. Before the angel Gabriel announces God's plan to bring the Messiah into the world through her, he says, "Do not be afraid, Mary; you have *found favor* with God."[1]

From the first words of greeting, God wants to assure Mary that He values her. She will be comforted by this if she will listen.

And just prior to *her* visitation, even Mary's cousin-in-law, an elderly priest, experiences a warm angel welcome: "Do not be afraid, Zechariah; *your prayer has been heard.*"

Yes, God had heard Zechariah, but Zechariah does not hear God. Neither does Mary. Or Daniel. Or Gideon. Instead of internalizing their divine affirmation, they rush right past it to get to the question of the hour: HOW.

"Pardon me, my lord," Gideon replies, "but *how* can I save Israel? My clan is the weakest in Manasseh, and I am the least in my family" (Judges 6:15).

Daniel asks, "*How* can I, your servant, talk with you, my lord? My strength is gone and I can hardly breathe" (Daniel 10:17).

"*How* will this be," Mary asks the angel, "since I am a virgin?" (Luke 1:34).

Zechariah asks the angel, "*How* can I be sure of this? I am an old man and my wife is well along in years" (Luke 1:18).

These God followers know themselves well. They can't see how a divine plan can work in their lives. In view of their glaring inadequacies, they have excuses on quick draw. Gideon basically says, *I am insignificant.* Daniel says, *I am weak.* Mary says, *I am unqualified.* And Zechariah says, *I am too late.*

Insignificant.

Weak.

Unqualified.

Too late.

Those are the same excuses we use today.

But God's word to them (and to us) is the opposite. He tells Gideon, *You say you are insignificant, but I say you are mighty.* He tells Daniel, *You say you are weak, but I say you are highly esteemed.* He tells Mary, *You say you are unqualified, but I say you have found favor.* He tells Zechariah, *You say you are too late, but I say you have been heard.*

We are so hasty to think that God does not hear us when we pray. The real problem is that we don't hear Him when He answers.

He explains this to the Israelites in Gideon's day. When they are wondering what they have done to merit hard time beneath the iron hand of Midianite invaders, God explains:

> *I brought you up out of Egypt, out of the land of slavery. I rescued you from the hand of the Egyptians. And I delivered you from the hand of all your oppressors; I drove them out before you and gave you their land. I said to you, "I am the LORD your God; do not worship the gods of the Amorites, in whose land you live." But you have not listened to me.* (Judges 6:8–10)

We often don't hear God because we are too busy listening to a darker voice. The one we call "the enemy" is not really *our* enemy. He is the enemy of God.

Jesus issues a good warning to His disciples and to us: "Do not be afraid of those who kill the body but cannot kill the soul. Rather, be afraid of the One who can destroy both soul and body in hell."[2]

We don't have to fear what Satan can do to temporal things. He will never be able to do anything without God's permission, and if God grants permission, then He will turn the trial into good for His own purposes. We *need* to be afraid of what Satan can do to eternal things.

Jesus reminds us that "the thief comes only to steal and

kill and destroy."[3] He is not insinuating that Satan's desire is to steal our belongings, to kill our bodies, and to destroy our livelihood in this temporal life. No, Satan seeks to steal, kill, and destroy in *everlasting* ways.

If we know that God's enemy does not concern himself with fleeting things, then read Isaiah 40:6–8 and identify what he *really* wants to target.

> *All people are like grass,*
> *   and all their faithfulness is like the flowers of the field.*
> *The grass withers and the flowers fall,*
> *   because the breath of the LORD blows on them.*
> *Surely the people are grass.*
> *The grass withers and the flowers fall,*
> *   but the word of our God endures forever.*

No, God's enemy doesn't seek to steal, kill, and destroy our possessions, our families, our jobs, our loved ones, or our dreams. All of that is just grass to him. He doesn't even seek to steal our joy, as we have often said. I used to proclaim this all the time, until I realized that I was becoming a little obsessed with the idea of not letting Satan steal my joy, as if that were something I needed to protect.

Joy is the fruit of the Holy Spirit, as are other attributes like faithfulness, self-control, and gentleness. People say, "Satan is trying to steal my joy!" but no one ever says, "Satan is trying to steal my gentleness!" I, for one, am often happy to let gentleness go. I don't hear anyone becoming concerned about the enemy stealing their faithfulness and self-control either, which are more dangerous spiritual characteristics to lose, really. Terrible things happen in a family when a spouse loses faithfulness. Many a regrettable path has been taken by an employee who has lost self-control.

But the enemy cannot have an effect upon the untouchable fruit of the Holy Spirit anyway. *We* are the only ones who limit the Spirit's fruitfulness in our lives. Either we "keep in step with the Spirit" or we do not.[4] The idea of Satan stealing our joy is nowhere in the Bible. The truth is, he doesn't even care about *our* joy. We, apart from God, are nothing to him. And *caring* is not one of his capabilities. He doesn't care about *anything*, least of all, our joy. His primary aim is not to make humans unhappy. Satan is not the Grinch.

His intentions are much worse. He seeks to steal, kill, and destroy the Word of God. By destroying the Word of God, he will hinder the continued work of God through humanity. This is the only strategy with everlasting consequence. He cannot defeat Jesus, so he goes after the Word. This has always been his strategy. Attacking the Word *is* attacking Jesus. The enemy knows that we have no chance against evil without the weapon of the Word in our hearts. He wants to knock that sword right out of our hands so that he can take us captive and separate us from God forever. His plan is not to steal *our* joy; it is to steal *God's* joy. Satan wants to keep the ones God loves away from Him forever.

He will *steal* the Word from us by insisting to us that we cannot memorize it and by busying our days so that we have no time to meditate on it. He will *kill* the Word for us by distracting us with trivia and legalism and by convincing us that it is boring and irrelevant. He will *destroy* the Word in us by twisting the truth in Scripture and by blinding us to all of the facets of God's character.

In the spiritual realm, it is so important to be empowered by the Word that the Lord gave explicit caution to the Israelites before they entered the Land of Canaan:

> *Be strong and very courageous. Be careful to obey all the instructions Moses gave you. Do not deviate from them, turning either to the right or to the left. Then you will be successful in everything you do. Study this Book of Instruction continually. Meditate on it day and night so you will be sure to obey everything written in it. Only then will you prosper and succeed in all you do.*[5]

Isn't it easy to see? God knows that when we are armed with Truth, we are not vulnerable to the father of lies. But when we let go of the Word, we are defenseless. Those who face a winter season without a full storehouse of provisions can be ruined by the bitter winds of difficulty. But those who have plenty of Truth put away in their heart will face the dark season with the confidence of knowing God for who He really is.

Winter in itself is not a bad thing. Think about how people take skiing vacations in the mountains of Colorado or Vermont. You don't have to be afraid of the snow. You can *enjoy* winter when you have what you need to survive it.

Look at the difference between a person who did not hold to the Word of God and One who did.

The serpent didn't go directly after Eve's joy in Eden. And if anyone had plenty of joy to steal, it was Eve. Look at her! She had killer gardening skills. She called God a close friend because they hung out together every day. Her body image was so good, she could walk around naked without a care. Her husband loved her like she was the only woman on earth. It's like they were *made* for each other.

Yet, when the enemy aimed at Eve, he didn't concern himself with the joy in her heart. He went after the Word in her heart. And because she hadn't listened closely enough and didn't know God's character well enough, Satan was able to dismantle the message that He had spoken.

Eve believed the father of lies instead of the Father of Lights.

In the same way, Satan didn't go directly after Jesus' joy during His time of testing, either. He went after the Word. And because Jesus had listened closely and knew it well, Satan couldn't touch God's Word in His heart. Jesus believed only what His Father had said.

When the enemy of God goes after us, he really goes after the Word in us. That is the way he weakens us. God has promised that He loves us; therefore, Satan sends adversity so we will stop believing that He does. God has assured us that He hears us; therefore, Satan sends tragedy so we will stop trusting that He does. God speaks Truth over us. Satan speaks nothing but lies over us. We must pay attention to One and not the other.

God tells us that we are *mighty*. He tells us that we are *highly esteemed*. He tells us that we *have found favor*. He tells us that we *have been heard*. In other words, God reminds us that we are made in His image. He is all of those things.

Satan tells us that we are *insignificant*. He tells us that we are *weak*. He tells us that we are *unqualified*. He tells us that we are *too late*. In other words, Satan tells us that we are made in *his* image. He is all of those things.

All of our worst descriptors describe the enemy, not us. He is powerless to change his destiny, so the best he can do is to make us doubt ours. We must familiarize ourselves with the Word of God so we can disregard any idea that is not in alignment with God's will.

We should behave differently than Pharisees. Jesus recognized that their hateful actions toward Him were the result of listening to the enemy's words instead of God's:

> *Why can't you understand what I am saying? It's because you can't even hear me! For you are the children of your father the devil, and you love to do the evil things he does. He was a murderer from the beginning. He has always hated the truth, because there is no truth in him. When he lies, it is consistent with his character; for he is a liar and the father of lies. So when I tell the truth, you just naturally don't believe me! Which of you can truthfully accuse me of sin? And since I am telling you the truth, why don't you believe me? Anyone who belongs to God listens gladly to the words of God. But you don't listen because you don't belong to God.*[6]

Jesus and Satan are heading in two different directions. Both of them are speaking over us every day. But Jesus is the only One headed toward hope.

We will follow who we listen to.

CHAPTER FIFTEEN

HE IS ENOUGH FOR YOU

No one has ever seen God; but if we love one another,
God lives in us and his love is made complete in us.

1 John 4:12

RUSS IS an award-winning teacher, tackling mathematics in a high school populated with some rough clientele. Yet my friend finds a way to penetrate even the toughest resistance to communicate caring and personal value to his students. By the end of a semester in his class, most students are not only willing to attempt difficult geometry problems, they find that they can excel at them.

He makes no secret of his success; the words he speaks are the difference. He writes of his deliberate attempt to speak life:

Last year I had a class that was very challenging. It was the last period of the day, and the students were easily distracted and off task. One particular student couldn't seem to stay in his seat and was a constant distraction. As my frustration increased, I found myself in conflict with these students almost daily. I began to realize that the more irritated I became, the more our classroom environment became less conducive to learning.

One morning I was thinking about this situation and decided to try a new strategy. I posted a banner that read, "You are bright, intelligent, and gifted. You are loved and accepted. You will succeed in all that you do!" That day I announced that they were my favorite class, that they were all gifted individuals, and that I considered it a privilege to teach them. At first they didn't believe me. They would scoff and say, "You say that to all your classes." I continued to speak this over them daily. I decided to declare what I wanted them to be, rather than focusing on the frustrations that I felt in dealing with how they were acting.

One day as I was teaching, I looked around to see the whole class engaged and working diligently on their assignment. I realized then that they had become what I had been speaking over them. They really *were* my favorite class.

• • •

This kind of teacher should not be rare. I wish we all would empower our students with our positive words.

I saw the power of negative words in students' lives when I worked as an English teacher at a public high school that fell into a lower socioeconomic bracket. Eighty-five percent of the student population was on free and reduced lunch, and that fact sometimes overshadowed everything else.

One year we had a winning football season, and the feeling of school spirit was unstoppable. The boys on the football team gave it their all every day on the practice field, and the student body rallied behind them in the hallways.

It disappointed us when a local newspaper reacted to our success by publishing an article that focused, not on the vision of the coaching staff or the skill of the players, but on the economic status of the campus. There were statistics about the meager incomes and painful financial situations of the families in our school zone, and every word of it hurt. The coaches tried to protect the team from reading the article, but news of it got around, as news does. I could sense a dark cloud that hadn't been on campus before.

But we continued to play well, right up to a play-off game against one of our most challenging opponents: a nearby school district that was known for the affluent and successful families represented in its population. Every year their football team was the best of the best. For them, state playoffs were a given from game one. They had too many perfect seasons to count. Our boys didn't have much of a chance against this team, and they knew it, but they still intended to play strong to the end.

Until negative words almost kicked them in the gut.

The Friday morning of the game, I arrived to work before sunrise to catch up on some essay grading. As I approached the campus in the dark, I noticed something strange in the light of the streetlamps. There was a thick white line on the brick of the building. As I drove closer, I could see that it was paper, hundreds of sheets of paper, wrapping *all the way* around the school. Someone had photocopied that hurtful article and taped it again and again, about chest high. They were reminding the boys of their poverty, stabbing them in their weakest spot.

When I walked inside the building, I saw Kathy, the head custodian and the school's biggest football fan, mobilizing her janitorial team. Her voice was intense as she directed each person, "You start by the west doors, and you start by the east. I will head out the south doors. Get every sheet of paper. *Every* sheet. Do you hear me? Don't miss *anything*. We have to get this down before the boys arrive in thirty minutes for morning practice. We can't let them see this. We can't let it crush them."

Kathy knew the power of words.

At the end of the day, I happened to see her, and she motioned for me to come look in the custodial closet, where she had hidden the ball she had made from all of the papers and packing tape they had pulled off the walls. It was at least four feet in diameter, as big as a boulder. She had said, "We can't let it crush them," and she was right. Someone had meant for those words to fall like a rock and smash our school's confidence to pieces.

Words contain muscle we cannot imagine. The Word of God tells us, "The tongue can bring death or life; those who love to talk will reap the consequences."[1] If only we could remember that the ability to kill or heal resides in our mouths. Maybe then, the person in the mirror would not meet the edge of our life-killing words. Most of us speak to ourselves in a way that we would never speak to another. So often, hurting ourselves with words is the *first* thing we do during a winter season, and it is the *worst* thing we do during a winter season. At the time we are most vulnerable, we are always tempted to turn words into a weapon and then turn that weapon onto ourselves.

I am the one to blame.

I am not worthy of anything else.

I am never going to get out of this.

I am old enough to know better by now.

I am finished.

I am . . .

If we say such sharp words to ourselves, we are missing the opportunity to speak life into our situations. The more we pour pain into already hurting hearts, the more we render ourselves less and less able to handle any difficulty. But there is something worse than all of this.

When we speak to ourselves this way, we are taking the name of the Lord in vain.

Recently I closed my morning prayer time with David's plea from Psalm 139:23–24: "Search me, God, and know my heart; test me and know my anxious thoughts. See if there is any offensive way in me . . ."

Then I waited to hear what He would say. The minutes grew.

Sometimes God speaks when I am not expecting Him to. Sometimes He doesn't speak when I am expecting Him to. Every time He speaks I am stunned by the mystery that He would actually utter His magnificent, star-wielding words to us. To *us*.

Suddenly, in the silence, His voice: *You have been taking My name in vain.*

"What?! I wouldn't, God!"

Confused, I couldn't think of an instance when I had taken His name in vain. I choose never to say the name of Jesus except to honor Him, praise Him, or pray to Him. I am deliberate in never saying, "Oh my God," or even saying or writing "OMG." As I was thinking this, He interrupted.

His voice: *My name is* I AM.

At this, the room flooded with every damaging phrase I had muttered inwardly over the last week, and all of it in *my* voice:

I am so stupid.

I am a failure.

I am hopeless.

I am fat.

I am old.

I am ugly.

I am trapped.

I am an idiot.

I am nobody.

Every statement began with "I am . . ." Every statement started with His name. It was a sacrilege I had never considered but could not deny. I bent low and asked for mercy.

• • •

When Great God introduces Himself to Moses from the flames, Moses wants to know His name.

> *Moses said to God, "Suppose I go to the Israelites and say to them, 'The God of your fathers has sent me to you,' and they ask me, 'What is his name?' Then what shall I tell them?"*
>
> *God said to Moses, "I AM WHO I AM. This is what you are to say to the Israelites: 'I AM has sent me to you.'"*
>
> *God also said to Moses, "Say to the Israelites, 'The LORD, the God of your fathers—the God of Abraham, the God of Isaac and the God of Jacob—has sent me to you.'*
>
> *"This is my name forever, the name you shall call me from generation to generation."*[2]

Today we refer to Him as *Lord, God, Father,* or *King,* and those terms describe His incomparable position or relationship. Those kinds of labels are connected to His name, the same way the labels of *teacher, daughter, sister,* or *friend* are connected to mine. Those terms describe my position or relationship. But my *name* is Nika.

In Isaiah 42:8, He says, "I am the LORD; that is my name!"

What if He is referring to that whole sentence as His name? He already told Moses that He is I AM. It brings new meaning to taking His name in vain.

We are never to use *any* term that refers to God—neither to His position nor to His name—in a less-than-holy way. He is the *only* Holy. He always is, always was, and always will be. The tricky part is realizing that eternal Deity chooses to live in human hearts instead of in anything made by human hands. It makes sense that He would prefer to live in something made by His hands, not ours.

When I need to remember this, I press my fingers to my temples. He lives there, inside. *We* are His temple. The Holy Spirit is forever rebuilding the temple in us. That is why when Jesus is the Cornerstone and God is the Master Architect of our lives, then no outside force can change the structure of our destiny. Even if the enemy throws a terrible brick in the veneer now and then, he cannot alter the architecture. We will always turn out as a temple. If we acknowledge God as we construct our lives, we become beautiful dwelling places for Him.

Galatians 2:20 tells us plainly, "I have been crucified with Christ. It is no longer I who live, but Christ who lives in me. And the life I now live in the flesh I live by faith in the Son of God, who loved me and gave himself for me."[3]

If I have accepted Christ, I no longer live. It is He who lives in me. So when I say, "I am stupid," to whom am I saying this? Every sentence that begins with the words "I am . . ." now jars me to clarity. If *I AM* is His name, then to begin a sentence this way is to address Him. To follow His name with harmful words such as *stupid, fat,* or *old* is to accuse, to insult, to devalue Him. How dare I? When I say "I am" I am saying "He is."

Some of us grieve over the practice of "cutting." It hurts to think that someone we love would slice their own skin as an expression of despair. Do you wonder how someone could bring themselves to the point of self-mutilation? That is a question to ask in the mirror. If you are like me, you cut yourself with sharp words daily. Will we never grieve over the blade of self-disdain?

The temptation to wound with words remains in me, as it may in you. But now I recognize damaging inner speech as a sly sin. It is so familiar to us that we allow it to sit, like garbage in the kitchen, until it starts to smell.

I'll take out the trash tomorrow morning, we think. Then we awaken in the night to a stench so bad it stings our nostrils. Trash talk cannot be removed fast enough. It is a slow, rotting blasphemy that will permeate our hearts. And God lives there, remember?

If we speak those wounding words to ourselves, we

are repeating lies about the Lord who made us in His very image.

Now when the temptation to "cut" arises, and I begin a sentence with "I am . . ." I have learned to stop myself just short of the knife's strike. He lives in me. So, I breathe and remember that when I talk to myself, I am talking to the I AM who chooses to live right here inside. Then I end my sentence with the truth about *Him*. I speak life into my situation, one true and faithful word at a time.

I am chosen.

I am worthy.

I am beautiful.

I am beloved.

I am enough.

Because, in His eyes, *I am*.

PART TWO
OUR CHARACTER

For if anyone is a hearer of the word and not a doer,
he is like a man observing his natural face in a mirror;
for he observes himself, goes away, and immediately
forgets what kind of man he was. But he who looks
into the perfect law of liberty and continues in it,
and is not a forgetful hearer but a doer of the work,
this one will be blessed in what he does.

James 1:23–25 NKJV

CHAPTER SIXTEEN

CHOOSE HUMILITY

*All of you, clothe yourselves with humility toward one
another, because, "God opposes the proudbut shows
favor to the humble." Humble yourselves, therefore, under
God's mighty hand, that he may lift you up in due time.
Cast all your anxiety on him because he cares for you.*

1 Peter 5:5–7

AFTER TOSSING the stuffed bear out of the second-story window, I crossed my arms in a snarky way and said, "If you like it so much, why don't you go get it?"

"Well, if you like this so much," my freshman roommate said, pointing to a pillow, "why don't you go get it?" With that, she threw my pillow out the window.

She and I still hadn't recovered from The Great Spaghettio Debacle.

"Oh, yeah? How about going to get *this*?" I taunted, ripping off her sheets, scooping all of her bed linens into my arms, and dropping them down to the sidewalk.

I put both hands on my hips, satisfied.

Then the fight really ignited. She ran to the desk, where my latest writing was in a folder. I dove for the framed photo of her boyfriend. We both hurried around the room, throwing each other's belongings through the window. It only lasted a few minutes before we heard a man's voice from outside.

"Ladies! Ladies, stop! What are you doing up there?"

"Oh no! It's the dean!" I whispered, dropping to the ground when I saw him. "What do we do?"

"Run!"

"Right, run! And hide! He won't know who did it! He doesn't know who we are!"

We both ran, laughing, to take cover in our friends' dorm rooms.

Not long after I had wedged myself under a bed, I heard someone announce that there was a man on the hall. I scooted closer to the wall, thinking I would just wait until the dean gave up and left the dorm.

Then he yelled my name.

"Nika Maples! Come here, right now! I am not leaving until you come out and speak with me."

My eyes grew wide. *How does he know my name?* Slowly, I emerged from my hiding place and reported to the dean in the dorm hallway. I couldn't figure out how he had deduced it was me who had been throwing things out of the window.

I stood in front of him for a moment before he extended his open palm to me. In it was my prescription medicine bottle.

"I think you dropped this, um . . . *Nika Maples*," he said, pointing to my name on the label.

• • •

Most of my life, I have wished for a common name, like Elizabeth or Ashley or Jennifer. Toy companies don't personalize bicycle plates for a kid named Nika. My name is not in a Top 40 song. It is not in a poem (What rhymes with Nika, anyway? You tell me). It is never printed on a souvenir keychain.

My name is only good for "The Name Game" song. *Nika-Nika-bo-bika, Banana-fanna-fo-fika.* That's all I've ever had.

Until now.

Just as I was finishing the manuscript for this book, I faced a mountain of doubt. I second-guessed myself for wanting to write it at all. I wasn't sure I had anything of worth to share with anyone who is going through a difficult time. I stopped writing for a few days.

I don't even like *writing about the dark season anymore,*

I said to myself one afternoon. *The idea of a spiritual winter is too silly. It doesn't even make any sense. I am going to ditch this project and start something else. There is no reason for another book about hope.*

That night I turned on the news.

The weather man was giving a report, and the banner at the bottom of the screen read: *Warning: Winter Storm Nika.*

Winter Storm *Nika*!

I was so excited to have an entire weather system named after me, that I laughed and texted my brother. I was thrilled!

But then I saw the footage. People in states far north of my mild Texas experience were not just feeling the cold. They were *fighting* the cold. With heads bowed in determination, they struggled even to walk through the snow and sleet of *Winter Storm Nika*. Then I wasn't thrilled anymore; I was motivated. Winter isn't silly. It's real. And it is hard.

• • •

There is a difference between these two stories. In the case of the storm with my name on it, the trouble was completely beyond my control. In the case of the medicine bottle with my name on it, I had brought the trouble on myself.

When difficulty comes with our name written all over it, we should drop to our knees in humility. That is the only sufficient response. From there, we can conduct a self-examination. In some cases, we have brought the trouble on ourselves, and it will be over as soon as we take corrective action. That was the situation for King Manasseh.

King Manasseh is one of my favorite people in the Old Testament, and I am thinking he is one of the first people I will try to talk to in heaven. I'll avoid the long lines to talk to the Apostle Paul or King David. I will just start with Manasseh. I don't think his appointment book will be full.

We meet Manasseh in the Bible and immediately learn that he is an evil king of Judah. This is evil in a horror-film kind of way. He interacts with the dead. He practices witchcraft. He has no sexual boundaries. He has a serious problem with substance abuse. He entices all the people of Judah to forsake Jehovah and worship idols. He brutally murders people he doesn't like (Jewish historians tell us that he had the prophet Isaiah publicly sawed in half). He brutally murders people he *does* like. He even sacrifices his own son in a fire. The Bible says that Manasseh "shed so much innocent blood that he filled Jerusalem from end to end."[1] How's that for a life legacy? Manasseh didn't worship God; he acted like he was a god.

His fatal move is to place an Asherah pole, an ancient idol, in the temple. That was the ultimate affront to the Holy One of Israel.

Jehovah had already given King Manasseh many chances. But "when God spoke to Manasseh and his people about this, they ignored him."[2] It was time to correct Manasseh for his disobedience. God said, "I will wipe out Jerusalem as one wipes a dish, wiping it and turning it upside down."[3] He was ready to clean house.

So "God directed the leaders of the troops of the king of Assyria to come after Manasseh. They put a hook in his nose, shackles on his feet, and took him off to Babylon."[4] This bullheaded king was led away like a bull.

Anyone who sets himself in the place of God in other people's eyes will be put in his proper place.

Ouch. Taking God's place is easier than you think. It doesn't always look like poorly ruling a kingdom. Honestly? In my life it looks like monitoring or correcting people *in my thoughts*. That is how Satan tempts me to play king. Maybe it is because I am a teacher by trade, but it is just as easy for me to grip a clipboard and a red pen in my head as it is for me to grip them in my hand.

Sure, I may be a teacher, but the Holy Spirit is The Teacher. Though I might like to apply to be His assistant, He is not hiring. When I am constantly observing the choices and behaviors of others, I am acting like God. And that is not my place. He watches. He corrects. He trains and disciplines His children. When I assume His position, I find that He turns His correction, training, and discipline toward *me*.

Sometimes discipline comes in the form of a storm. It shows up like trouble with my name on it.

But there is only one purpose for that kind of dark season, and it is not punishment, as we see in the rest of Manasseh's story. After being dragged by a hook in his nose to prison, he finally saw the error of his thinking. He did the only thing he could do: "*He went to his knees in prayer* asking for help—total repentance before the God of his ancestors. As he prayed, GOD was touched; GOD listened and brought him back to Jerusalem as king. That convinced Manasseh that GOD was the One in control."[5]

Manasseh learned to live on his knees, and that is when God brought him to his feet.

Can you believe that God forgave Manasseh after all that bloodshed? Can you believe He restored a murderer's royal throne? What an amazing God we serve. We cannot comprehend the depth of His mercy. No, trials are never a punishment from His hand. But there are occasions when they might be discipline. There is a difference. Punishment is final; with discipline there's a do-over. If we change our course and choose humility, many times He restores what we have lost.

Manasseh's winter began with his actions, and his counteractions were the beginning of his spring. More than one dark season in my life was brought about by stubborn pride, by unbelief, or by something else that necessitated correction.

Therefore, I am still trying to work out Philippians 2:3–4 in my daily life. What does it look like to "do nothing out of selfish ambition or vain conceit? Rather, in humility value others above yourselves, not looking to your own interests but each of you to the interests of the others"? What does it look like to live on my knees?

I try to start there in the morning. The physical act of getting on my knees reminds me who is in control. I get on my knees to pray in the morning because the rest of my day will follow suit. Actually, the entirety of my character will follow suit. And it will take good character to accomplish the "good works, which God prepared in advance for us to do."[6] Sometimes trials are what is needed to build that character into us because we establish meaningful spiritual habits when we are uncomfortable.

Choosing humility is the first spiritual habit of a hope hunter. The practice of choosing humility will add nothing to our schedules. It only takes a few seconds to get on our knees as we switch off our alarm in the morning. It only takes a few seconds to raise our hands in surrender in the closet before we get dressed. It only takes a few seconds to look out the kitchen window as we pour our coffee and say, "The day I'm about to live is Yours, God. You made it, and it is Yours. All of it. Today is not about me." It only takes a few seconds to open our palms in our laps before we start the car to go to work. No matter the manifestation of our morning moment of humility, the rest of the day will bend to that decision. Then, later in the morning or afternoon, when there comes an opportunity to take a prideful stance, we will already have established "downward momentum." We will think twice before we choose anything other than humility. We will look for opportunities to serve or to make other people look good rather than ourselves.

Under God's mighty hand, we can relax because we know He will lift us up in due time. We do not have to lift up ourselves. I opened this chapter with a verse that promises that very thing, which is beautifully restated in *The Message*: "So be content with who you are, and don't put on airs. God's strong hand is on you; he'll promote you at the right time. Live carefree before God; he is most careful with you."[7]

God is most careful with us. Maybe that is one reason He wants us to choose humility. He knows that pride precedes a fall.[8]

And He knows that people who are already on their knees don't trip.

CHAPTER SEVENTEEN

GIVE GRACE

A person's wisdom yields patience;
it is to one's glory to overlook an offense.

Proverbs 19:11

THE OLD MAN in the pearl snap shirt held the door for me. He waited while I negotiated the broken places in the sidewalk and leaned on my cane. When I approached the entrance to the mall, I was about to tell him how handsome his plaid shirt was, but he tipped his cowboy hat and spoke first.

"You walk like 'at on purpose?"

This took me by surprise. "What? Well . . . no, sir. I don't."

"Whew. Sure glad it's you and not me," he said.

I told him his shirt was handsome anyway.

I gave him grace.

• • •

One lonely lemon rolled down the side of the produce pyramid at the neighborhood grocery store. Then it leaped heroically, only to miss my shopping basket on my motorized mart cart and land on the polished floor.

I had parked the mart cart parallel to the row of citrus, and the lemon had fallen right down into the two-foot-wide ravine between my bumper and the produce stand. Instinctively, I reached for it, and that was when my world slowed to sludge the way it always does when I am falling.

Who falls out of a *parked* mart cart?

This girl.

Securely wedged between the cart and the produce, I lay on the grocery store floor like a corpse, arms crossed and pinned to my chest, Dracula-style. Underneath me? The lemon. It brings new meaning to the term *fresh squeezed*. Above me? A tenuous tower of fruit threatened to avalanche.

Then the story really goes sour.

Four couples—as in eight people—walked right past me. They saw me too. Oh yes, they saw. Couple #1 was beside me, close enough to trip on my limp, cadaver-looking foot. I craned my neck and looked up at them with pleading eyes. You know when you can *tell* someone is trying not to look at you? They must take their organic oranges seriously, because they almost needed a magnifying glass, the way they examined those navels. Couple #2 was selecting wine. The gentleman, and I use this term loosely here, looked in my direction and we locked eyes for three seconds. In a grocery store, a three-second stare is a *long* time. Then it was like he suddenly heard:

On your mark . . . get set . . . merlot!

Bam, he turned back to the bottle in his hand. What was going through his mind, I wonder, as he saw me lying there on the linoleum like I was in a mausoleum? Did he think I was doing emergency meditation? Stop, drop, and yoga? Couples #3 and #4 cruised by and had to steer their brimming buggies around my mart cart in order to make it down the slim aisle. Again there was eye contact.

For all they knew, I was dead. You should be afraid of the fact that nobody does anything about a carcass in the grocery store these days.

I don't know why I didn't call out for help; by then I was just too irritated. I wanted them to *want* to help. It took me two or three minutes of maneuvering to push the cart an inch. I had to heave it sideways with my shoulder before I could ease myself upright and uncross my arms. Miraculously, I did this without completely splitting the lemon with my shoulder blade. Somehow, I used my knees, then my feet, to push the cart a few inches. I was grunting and panting until I was back on my feet. During the whole thing, a few people walked past, obviously thinking something like, *Handicapped woman down! Look away!*

As I dusted off my jeans, I whispered through my teeth, "This is just an exercise . . . This is just an exercise . . ." Then, though it took great strength to keep the sarcasm off my face, I took a deep breath, looked up, and actually smiled a real smile.

I gave them grace.

•   •   •

The August sun scorched the pavement, and I had been walking as fast as I could to get into the cool air of the church building. It didn't surprise me when I fell to the floor just inside the doors.

Somehow, I ended up on my back. The aluminum lip of the threshold pressed into my spine, and I lay there, too stunned to move. The brilliant sky almost blinded my view, but I could make out a woman running to me with her hand outstretched.

"Nika! Nika!" she yelled.

When she reached my side, her body blocked the sun, and I could see her big grin. I was happy to see her too, though I didn't recognize her. I leaned up a bit in order to take her hand.

"You *are* Nika, right? Nika Maples?" She shook my

hand, barely taking a breath before continuing, "Goodness, I can't believe this moment is really happening! I have been waiting for a chance to talk to you, and here it is! You spoke at my school district's convocation last year, and I wanted to tell you how much your message meant to me, but I could not get down to the front to talk to you afterward, so I left. But ever since then, I have been praying that God would give me another chance to speak with you, so I could thank you! It is like He gave me a gift today!"

"I am glad you were encouraged." I smiled up at her. "That is good to hear."

She let go of my hand, saying, "I was! I was encouraged! Thank you so, so much! Your words meant the world to me. God bless you! Have a great day!"

And then she walked away, leaving me there in the doorway.

"God bless you too!" I called after her sincerely.

I gave her grace.

• • •

Living with disability has been a powerful spiritual blessing because it gives me so many opportunities to give grace. Not that I want to, or even *can* by myself. But Christ has given so much grace to me that it spills over if I let it.

During those times when it is difficult to give grace,

I hear one of my mother's frequent phrases in my head. I used to talk with her after school, complaining about this rude friend or that unkind teacher, threatening to speak my mind to them the next day. But no matter what difficult person I encountered when I was young, my mother would always caution me, "Nika, be gracious." There were days when this suggestion irritated me! I wanted her permission to retaliate. Now that I am an adult, I cannot think of a time when I have regretted a gracious response, yet I have regretted plenty of ungracious ones.

Self-defense is a reflex. Our human inclination is to strike back, dishing out the same treatment we have received. But Jesus says, "If someone strikes you, stand there and take it."[1] This doesn't feel like the right thing to do, but it is. Only through steel-eyed spiritual surrender can we resist the urge to act as a mirror-image to those who hurt us.

From maturity, we will respond with different actions than the ones we have received. From adolescence, we will respond in kind.

High-schoolers in my English classroom have said so many times that they will show respect to such-and-such a teacher when that teacher shows respect to them. That they will start taking their parents seriously when their parents start taking them seriously. That they will work hard at their jobs when they see their boss work just as hard.

Adolescents think they appear confident and in control when they say these things. They do not realize how insecure and juvenile they sound.

The person with inner strength respects others because he respects God. He takes others seriously because he takes God seriously. He works hard because he is working for God. Our choices should have nothing to do with what we see and everything to do with what we don't. Treating others better than they deserve feels unnatural. In fact, it requires *super*natural self-control.

It can be hard enough to exercise self-control on a good day. It is even harder if you are low and have been weakened by winter. But I can almost guarantee that it is precisely when you are down on the ground that you are most likely to be kicked.

Like it or not, giving grace is the second spiritual habit of a hope hunter.

How can you give grace?

Giving grace requires having grace. That is why the picture of grace is a pitcher of grace. The more we are filled with the grace of Jesus, the easier it is to pour grace onto others.

• • •

One night, Jesus is eating dinner in the home of Simon, and an uninvited prostitute interrupts to create a mighty awkward moment. She kneels. She cries. She kisses Jesus' feet. She anoints His holy toes with perfume.

The host of the house is annoyed with the woman *and* with Jesus. He thinks to himself, "If this man was the prophet I *thought* he was, he would have known what kind of woman this is who is falling all over him."[2]

Is it any surprise that Simon has no grace for the sinful woman? He has no grace for Jesus Himself! Someone who cannot give grace, cannot give it to *anyone*, even to someone who has never done anything wrong. (There is a people pleaser out there who needs to read that again. Swallow it whole: there are some people you will *never* be able to please.)

Jesus shocks the room when He defends the prostitute: "'I tell you, her sins—and they are many—have been forgiven, so she has shown me much love. But a person who is forgiven little shows only little love.' Then Jesus said to the woman, 'Your sins are forgiven.'"[3]

Look at the way Simon would not show grace to the One who deserved it, but Jesus showed grace to the one who *didn't* deserve it. I want to be like Jesus. Oh, but wait. Now that I think about it, that means there might be more and more people who don't deserve grace showing up in my life. The kind of people who say rude things and do things that hurt. I don't like admitting that Jesus didn't try to avoid them. Steering clear was not His aim. It's almost like He *looked* for reasons to be with grace-needy people.

Maybe He spent time with the ones who needed grace because giving grace was His whole agenda. Yes, Jesus spends time with people who need grace, and that is why He spends time with me. Not because I am doing it all right, but because it is so easy for me to mess things up.

I still say, "I want to be like Jesus," but I say it with a shaky voice, aware of the ways it will push me. Grace will have to be my whole agenda too. The next time someone messes things up, I am going to have to remind myself that I said I wanted this, an opportunity to be like Jesus.

But I also want to have the attitude of the prayerful prostitute in the story. Simon kicked her while she was down. She was physically low because she was kneeling at that moment, but she was emotionally low because she was grieving for her sins. I am astonished that she was able to ignore Simon. She didn't even look at him. She did not turn her eyes toward the condemning crowd in the room. She did not flee in shame. She did not react in self-defense.

She stayed at the feet of Jesus and never took her eyes off Him.

She let Him be the One to defend her.

This woman was able to give grace to Simon because Jesus had given so much to her. Her heart was full of God's grace, and she couldn't help but pour it out. The saddest part of the story is that this is where it ends. We don't see any transformation in Simon. With Jesus in the room, there was enough grace to fill more than just the heart of one prostitute. There was enough to fill Simon as well. We are left to wonder if he ever knelt to receive it. But first he would have to admit how much he needed it, and I am not sure he was ready to do that.

When grace is difficult for us to give to others, it indicates a grace shortage in our hearts. It tells us we have an empty pitcher. Ask God to remind you how much grace you have been given.

He can refill you.

CHAPTER EIGHTEEN

SING TRUTH

The LORD is my strength and my shield;
My heart trusted in Him, and I am helped;
Therefore my heart greatly rejoices,
And with my song I will praise Him.

Psalm 28:7 NKJV

ANY PUBLIC SCHOOL TEACHER knows that the morning of the state-mandated test dawns with mixed emotions. On one hand, there is tension. There is the greater tension of hoping that we have done as much as we possibly could to prepare our students when they arrive with sharpened pencils in hand. And there is also the smaller tension of wondering whether *that one student* will bother to show up to school at all.

On the other hand, there is relief. There is the greater relief of realizing that whatever is going to happen is going to happen. Nothing more can be done. And there is also the smaller relief of knowing that our exhausting tutoring schedules have come to an end.

(Okay, maybe that kind of relief is not small.)

A few years ago, I had an added emotion on the morning of the exam: panic. The night before, I had been walking from the driveway to my front door, and my toe just hit the edge of the sidewalk instead of landing squarely upon it. When I fell, I twisted my ankle in such a way that I almost could not stand up and make it inside the house. After applying ice and taking some aspirin, I went to sleep.

The next morning, I pulled back the sheet, looked at my elephantine ankle, and decided it must be fractured. By the time I got dressed, the pain was so intense it was affecting my ability to concentrate. I couldn't put any weight on that foot. I hopped into the school building where I taught sixth grade and said something to my principal that she'd probably imagined in her nightmares. Just one hour before the state test, I told her I didn't think I could stay to administer it. I couldn't walk around the room to monitor; I couldn't even think straight. There was a moment of behind-the-scenes strain, and then another teacher who had been trained on the testing procedures was able to take my place.

At the doctor, an X-ray revealed that my ankle was not broken, and I almost protested that there had been a mistake. I couldn't believe it. I was *sure* it was broken! The physician just gave me a plastic boot to secure my ankle for six weeks and sent me home.

Teaching can be the most joyful job in the world, but some circumstances make it miserable. A foot injury is one of them.

Do you know how to turn crazy kids into calm ones? Walk around the room constantly. You can enjoy stellar behavior if you will make the rounds, touching a shoulder here and there, and smiling as you point to the work to keep a student on task. This is the way the teacher owns the classroom.

Do you know how to turn calm kids into crazy ones? Sit at your desk with your foot propped up on ice. If you teach from a chair, the students will own the classroom.

Behavior became ridiculous.

By the end of the fifth week, I felt so exasperated about going to work that I moaned as I got out of my car in the morning to head inside, and it wasn't because of ankle pain. My attitude was so bad, I had begun snapping at students, which only made them act worse. Finally, I had to put an end to the downward spiral, which was entirely my fault. I called a class meeting and we put down our work. I told a student to turn off the harsh florescent lights overhead while I pulled up the blinds and let in the afternoon sun.

I went to the front of the room, sat on the stool beside my podium, and sighed. Then I smiled, something they hadn't seen in a long time. I apologized for taking out my frustration on them for more than a month. They apologized to me for being disruptive. It was a nice moment of honesty and solidarity, during which one girl said something that reverberated in my heart for weeks.

I had asked the class, "Well, I will be getting rid of this horrid boot soon, so let's try to rewind to the place where we first went wrong so that we can start over together. The initial days after my accident, things were fine, but then they plummeted soon afterward. At what moment did you notice that something about our class personality was off?"

Everyone shrugged.

But McKenzie raised her hand. "Um . . . Ms. Maples? I guess I knew something was wrong when you stopped singing," she said quietly.

I wouldn't have thought of it myself, but that is exactly the moment when things started to deteriorate. I have a habit of singing out some of my simple instructions in class, which makes fifth- and sixth-grade students laugh and high school students roll their eyes goodnaturedly. I sing when radio songs are stuck in my head. I sing at recess. I sing on the way to the cafeteria. The kids join in softly. When we all work hard, stay focused, and finish our assignments quickly, we even take a short break to have a karaoke moment or an all-together sing-along to a fun pop song. Singing keeps a smile on my face. The moment my singing stopped, so did my smile.

That experience in the classroom is a microcosm of life. Actions informed my attitude then, and they still do. I felt bad physically, but then I started acting bad, and that made me feel even worse. If I had kept singing, there might have been a faster recovery time . . . at least for my heart, if not for my ankle.

The third spiritual habit of a hope hunter may stretch those of us who have a strong inhibition muscle. We can change our perspectives during winter if we sing truth. You don't necessarily have to sing out loud in front of other people, but you do have to sing out loud.

One of my friends tells me that he has a practice most nights before he goes to bed. He says aloud, "I am not the one in control of my life. God is the One in control of my life."

When I asked him why he says it *out loud*, he explained, "Because sometimes my ears need to hear my mouth say what my heart believes."

In other words, just thinking of God's greatness may not be enough. We may need to say it. We may need to sing it.

And we can't sing just anything either. We have to sing truth. That can be a challenge for me on certain days. Believe me, if there were a televised contest called *So You Think You Can Sing All the Radio Hits*, I would be a contender. I easily memorize lyrics, and I learn songs quickly. But I have to be careful. If a new song is catchy, I can find myself singing some lyrics that reflect the opposite of what I know is true. Yet my ears need to hear my mouth sing what my heart believes, so I am more diligent about that than I used to be. Now, though it pains me to turn off an irresistibly good tune or beat because the lyrics are crude and not God-honoring, I do it, switching to a station with music that reiterates God's goodness instead. It is a practical way to choose light over darkness.

Sometimes we are hurting so badly, we could not give a rock-solid, faith-firm answer if somebody asked us what we believe, but we can always sing along with the truth-laden lyrics someone else has written. We can sing songs of truth. On a lot of days, that is enough.

You may ask, "Why can't I just speak truth? Do I have to *sing* it?"

We should definitely be speaking truth. But singing engages something deep inside. It opens us. It wakes us. Singing readies our spirits like nothing else.

I would never suggest that we be superficial and put

on a saccharin smile when our heart aches. That is not anywhere close to what I mean. It is not helpful to pretend as if feelings do not exist. I believe that feelings should be deeply felt, rather than ignored. But there are natural actions we can take that will bring healing to our emotions, and one of them is singing praise. The lower we feel, the more we should lift Him on high.

When I am busy hunting hope, though, it is hard to remember to sing.

My friends, we cannot afford to stop. It has never been more important to remember how good He is.

For now, we may not see the purpose of the dark seasons. We do not have Divine perspective. Though we do not see all that God sees, we can be sure of the fact that He sees *us*.

We may be in the dark season, but there is no sweeter sound than *Noël*, a carol sung in winter. One day, the wind will stop. One day, the Bright Morning Star will dawn. One day, the shadows will be no more.

Until then, our ears need to hear our mouths sing what our hearts believe.

CHAPTER NINETEEN

KEEP GOING

---

*I don't mean to say that I have already achieved
these things or that I have already reached perfection.
But I press on to possess that perfection for which Christ Jesus
first possessed me. No, dear brothers and sisters, I have not
achieved it, but I focus on this one thing: Forgetting the past
and looking forward to what lies ahead, I press on to reach
the end of the race and receive the heavenly prize for
which God, through Christ Jesus, is calling us.*

Philippians 3:12–14 NLT

ON CHRISTMAS EVE, I had one more stocking stuffer to buy before I was finished with my Christmas shopping. My sister-in-law had been wanting to try a certain kind of nail polish. I had planned to get it for her, but I kept forgetting. Then, on a hectic day like December 24th, I braved the crowds one last time. The first store was sold out, so I went to another store. If I couldn't find it there, I decided, I would have to get it for her after Christmas.

When I walked in, I knew I was out of luck. The cosmetic shelves looked like the bread aisle at a Dallas grocery store when snow is in the forecast. People had ransacked the shelves in last-minute desperation. They had left the displays in shambles. It looked like just about every woman was going to get nail polish in her stocking. There was hardly any left.

I made a circuit three times, just to make sure there wasn't a stray bottle of the kind I needed. On my final loop, I noticed a woman on her knees, concentrating as she sorted through some cosmetics.

"Excuse me, ma'am? Do you work here?"

She nodded.

I explained my last-minute mission, but she never spoke. She led me to another aisle, then she just pointed and nodded. When the polish wasn't there, I thanked her for her help and chuckled that I was just going to have to give up on that gift.

She didn't smile back.

I turned and started to walk away, when I suddenly felt a nudge in my heart to go talk to her. I spun around and blurted the sudden question that came to me, "Ma'am? Excuse me? Do you mind if I ask where you are from?"

"Egypt," she said flatly.

"Welcome! I am so glad you are here! How long have

you been here in Texas?" The Holy Spirit kept urging me to talk to her as the Christmas Eve crowds moved around us.

"A year."

"Oh, do you enjoy it here? I mean, did you *want* to come to America?"

"No, I *had* to come here. They are killing Christians in Egypt, and before we could flee, they cut off my son's hand."

I gasped. For the first time, she showed emotion. Her face contorted in grief, and she looked away. We had barely started a conversation, and instantly she was thrown into a vulnerable place she hadn't expected to go while at work.

"Oh, no!" I whispered. "I am so sorry. Is he alive? Did he live?"

"Yes, he is here in Texas with me. But it is hard," she said, wiping a tear and looking back at the pile of nail polish. She didn't want to talk anymore, not there, not then. So we just ended the conversation abruptly.

I had been in a wonderful mood that day. Everything was in order in my world. When I had pulled back the bed covers that morning, I had been eager to experience all the Christmas Eve traditions: hot chocolate, Christmas lights, and laughter. As I was putting on my shoes, I had never imagined that they would take me to a drugstore aisle, where I would be entrusted with someone's breaking heart. I was instantly humbled and didn't know what to say or do.

There are many things I could have said and done, but I froze, blinking hard, watching her turn back to the pile of cosmetics on the floor. I wish I had knelt down to pray with her. I wish I had invited her to be with my family on Christmas day. I wish I had asked if she had any current needs. I wish I had given her my phone number. I wish I had asked her if she had found a church home yet. I wish I had asked if her son was going to school or working and had friends or a place to belong. I wish I had asked if he needed rehabilitation assistance. I wish I had asked if she had other family members in danger in Egypt. I could think all day about the things I wish I had done. I did none of the things I should have. All I did was thank her and walk away.

But I couldn't just walk away.

At the check-out counter, I felt my throat closing off and my eyes filling with tears. I couldn't leave the store and get on with my merry Christmas as if I had never seen a sister in pain. I grabbed two restaurant and clothing store gift cards off the rack by the register and added them to my purchases.

A couple of gift cards didn't fix anything for her, but I went back and gave them to her before leaving the store. "Please . . . I have a gift for you," I said, touching her shoulder. "Merry Christmas . . . Merry Christmas. I know it must be hard. But God loves you so."

She put down the lipsticks and cried as she leaned to embrace me.

"God loves you. He loves you so, so much. He sees you. He hears you," I said in her ear, hugging her tight.

Then she wiped her face and returned to her work. I left the store, trembling.

Somewhere, for someone, it is *always* winter. We can't be content just to hunt for hope for ourselves. We have to hunt for the people around us as well. Everywhere we go, we walk by people who shiver with cold. We pass people who carry a weighty darkness. There are a thousand Christians in a thousand places who are trying hard to keep their minds on their work, just so they don't have to hear the shattering of their hearts.

In the *The Lion, the Witch, and the Wardrobe*, the woodland creatures say that it is "Always winter, *never* Christmas" in Narnia. In our world, it may be winter, but—glory!—it's always Christmas because Christ has come to the masses.

Christ has come so that we might have Light in our darkness:

For God, who said, "Let there be light in the darkness," has made this light shine in our hearts so we could know the glory of God that is seen in the face of Jesus Christ.

213

We now have this light shining in our hearts, but we ourselves are like fragile clay jars containing this great treasure. This makes it clear that our great power is from God, not from ourselves.

We are pressed on every side by troubles, but we are not crushed. We are perplexed, but not driven to despair. We are hunted down, but never abandoned by God. We get knocked down, but we are not destroyed. Through suffering, our bodies continue to share in the death of Jesus so that the life of Jesus may also be seen in our bodies.[1]

Why do we suffer? Because we live in a fallen world. The only sensible reason we can take heart in the darkness is because Jesus has overcome this world.[2] That is why, even now, we can find His Light when our lives are dark. We will see the spring we seek. Winter won't last forever.

This really *is* a season. And seasons change.

That is why the fourth spiritual practice of a hope hunter is to keep going. No matter what. To keep going toward the heart of God. In every way possible.

I know that spring will come for the Egyptian woman in the drugstore because Christ is here with her, and knowing Him makes all the difference. In His strength, she uprooted her family and moved to another country. She is earning a living, and for now, she and her son are safe. She is already on her way, making steps toward a better day. But I can't help thinking how much work she has left to do even though she has escaped immediate danger. Every day she must choose to keep going. Sometimes when we dream of spring, we think it will be a time of total release and peace. We long to cross over into the promised land. Until recently, I didn't realize how much work is required even in the promised places.

• • •

When Moses leads the Israelites to the brink of the Promised Land, they still have a lot of work left to do. They must cross the Jordan River to claim all of the land beyond the west bank. Then they must displace the Canaanite people. There are many battles ahead of them. But they are already weary from their wilderness wandering. The tribes of Reuben and Gad are so tired, in fact, that they decide to stop right where they are. They ask Moses if they can go ahead and claim the land east of the Jordan River and call it a day. Moses stops what he is doing to turn to them in disbelief. After all of their hardship, the Reubenites and Gadites are ready to quit just short of the finish line. I can picture their leader's frustrated voice as he starts, "'Do you intend to stay here while your brothers

HUNTING HOPE

go across and do all the fighting?' Moses asked the men of
Reuben and Gad. 'Why do you want to discourage the rest
of the people of Israel from going across to the land the
LORD has given them?'"[3]

To keep going has never been more important than that
moment, but the Reubenites and Gadites don't want to do
it. They have had enough. They see how much fighting
there is left to do and they are ready to quit.

Eventually, Moses lets the two tribes have the eastern
land they asked for, but only on the condition that they
leave their wives and children settled there while their men
forge the river to join the fight.

I can't help thinking of the Reubenites and Gadites in
the context of my own life. So many times I find myself
ready to stop just short of the promised land because I am
so tired from the effort it took to get there. What a mistake
that would be. But it is also a mistake to think that there
will ever be a carefree day in our lives. The promised land
is a provision that God has made for us. It is the best place
and best way we are to live. In our promised land, we will
be free. But we will not be free from work.

Even Adam and Eve had work to do in Eden. Gardens
require maintenance. I am convinced that we will even have
work to do in heaven. But it will not be toil, as it is so
often here. There, it will be rewarding work. In *The Divine*

Conspiracy, Dallas Willard suggests that "we should expect that in due time we will be moved into our eternal destiny of creative activity with Jesus and his friends and associates to the 'many mansions' of 'his Father's house.'"

> Thus we should not think of ourselves as destined to be celestial bureaucrats, involved eternally in celestial "administrivia." That would be only slightly better than being caught in an everlasting church service. No, we should think of our destiny as being absorbed in a tremendously creative team effort, with unimaginably splendid leadership, on an inconceivably vast plane of activity, with ever more comprehensive cycles of productivity and enjoyment.[4]

The promised land is hard work, but it is good work. And it is worth the work. Don't stop on this side of it.

Keep going.

CHAPTER TWENTY

WAIT EXPECTANTLY

Don't be misled: No one makes a fool of God. What a person
plants, he will harvest. The person who plants selfishness,
ignoring the needs of others—ignoring God!—harvests a crop
of weeds. All he'll have to show for his life is weeds! But the
one who plants in response to God, letting God's Spirit do the
growth work in him, harvests a crop of real life, eternal life.
So let's not allow ourselves to get fatigued doing good.
At the right time we will harvest a good crop if we don't give
up, or quit. Right now, therefore, every time we get
the chance, let us work for the benefit of all, starting with
the people closest to us in the community of faith.

Galatians 6:7–10 MSG

IN COLLEGE, my friend DeeAnn let someone borrow
her car. He was planning to go repelling at a state park four
hours away. DeeAnn had given her life to the Lord for the
first time only a few months earlier, and she welcomed the

opportunity to share with others. She wouldn't be needing her car that weekend anyway.

When her friend returned from the trip, she smiled to greet him and said, "How'd it go?"

He said he had good news and bad news. The good news was that everyone in the group had made it home safely. The bad news was that her car hadn't. The keys had fallen out of his pocket somewhere on their expedition. Her car was still locked up in the parking lot of the state park.

Instead of panicking, DeeAnn carefully considered what to do. She thought about calling a locksmith, but she was a college student who had only recently come out of the foster care system and she had no money to her name. She didn't even have anyone she could call for financial help. She thought through every possible option, and finally decided upon the most difficult one.

"I'll wait. I'll just wait. I may be new to this faith thing, but if I'm reading the Bible correctly, it seems like waiting is one of the most important things a Christian can do." Maybe money for a locksmith would come somehow. Maybe there would be an answer that she could not anticipate. She couldn't explain it, but she felt peace in her heart about waiting.

So she prayed. And she waited.

A hard rain started the following morning. It rained so much there was a flash flood warning. It rained for four days straight. It rained all across the state.

After the rain cleared, another group of friends that had no connection to the first group of repellers said that they were making a weekend hiking and repelling trip, and they asked DeeAnn if she would like to go. She said yes before she learned it would be a trip to the same state park where her friend had been the week before. At least once, her car keys crossed her mind, but the park was enormous, and the "gully washer" they'd had for four days had most certainly swept the keys away. She looked forward to the hike as a simple time to get away, have fun, and spend time with God out in nature. She continued to feel peace about leaving her problems at the feet of the Lord. She waited expectantly for Him to act.

The weekend weather was perfect. DeeAnn and her friends enjoyed a spectacular trip. On the last descent of the weekend, she stopped halfway down to rest on a precipice high above the canyon. A friend stopped to take in the view with her. They talked about the school year and their hopes for the summer. They talked about God and His faithfulness in their lives.

Then her friend blurted, "Hey, wouldn't it be weird if you found your car keys out here?"

DeeAnn shrugged and was about to answer when she happened to see metal glint in the sunlight. There were her keys, sitting on a rock within reach. Just like that.

The storm had not washed the keys away. Jesus had honored her waiting and made them stay.

• • •

When facing challenges, we always look to Jesus for answers, thinking He will tell us to *do* something. Often, what He tells us to do is wait. We do not have to wait in resignation. No, we wait in expectation. We surrender in glad wonder, as the anonymous writer describes from God's perspective in *God Calling*: "Resignation to My Will keeps me barred out from more hearts than does unbelief. Can anything be such a crime against Love as being resigned? My Will should be welcomed with a glad wonder if I am to do My Work in the heart and life."[1]

This is the way we wait for spring, with the expectancy of a hunter's heart. The last, the most important, spiritual practice of a hope hunter is to wait expectantly.

We can live in the expectation of spring because it *will* come. Even during dark days, we must operate in the anticipation of a dawn. Every gardener knows that if he waits too long to plant, it will be too late. Tulip and daffodil bulbs are buried deep in the ground before the frost, so that we can have blooms much later in the spring.

Do not be someone who gets so caught up in the dark season that you never prepare to leave it. Some people seem to thrive in a crisis. They may have experienced a snowy season one time, and ten years later, they are still wearing ski clothes. Maybe they are motivated by the sympathy or the admiration of others, but they linger in winter because they believe there is no other way for them to live. At times, I have been tempted to do this too, thinking extreme endurance is an accomplishment. But painful experiences don't make anyone better than anyone else, and we have to be careful not to think so.

There are times when groups invite me to tell of God's faithfulness through suffering in my life. It is a story I love to tell. He has been so good. Afterward, when it is someone else's turn, people indicate an apprehension about sharing their own testimony.

"My story isn't very interesting. I haven't been through as much as she has," they say.

This reaction bothers me so much. Everyone's story is valuable because everyone's story is God's story. We will defeat the enemy "by the blood of the Lamb and the word of [our] testimony," by retelling what God has done in our lives.[2] God does so much for us daily that we should have a new testimony to tell every day. A story laced with pain is not more valuable than a story without it. That is why, at times, I choose to tell a version of my testimony that does not involve the dramatic hospital scenes I have survived. *Every* moment in my life proves God's faithfulness, not just the winter ones. The spring and summer days speak of Him too.

Do not let yourself be defined by one suffering season for the rest of your life. I eventually had to grow out of that tendency. It helped that my mother had the same response every time I used setbacks as an excuse when I was growing up.

"Aw, quit playing poor mouth," she'd say, waving her hand and ushering me onto a more productive topic of conversation than complaining.

You and I are so much more than what has happened to us. It is time to quit playing poor mouth. It might be time to tell a new story.

You are not *the sick person*. You are not *the divorced person*. You are not *the unemployed person*. You are not *the depressed person*. You are not *the person with anxiety*. You may have lived through a season of sickness, divorce, unemployment, depression, or anxiety, or you may be there still, but you don't have to let that label stick forever in front. The label is not your name. Your identity is bigger than the facts of your life. You don't have to act like winter takes all.

You are not winter.

And winter is not your only season. Joy will give you the strength to walk out of it. The Word tells us we can count on it: "Don't be dejected and sad, for the joy of the LORD is your strength!"[3]

Grasp the joy of the Lord, and you will grasp strength. Grasp strength, and you will watch the atmosphere transform *even during the difficulty*. The Valley of Weeping can become a place of renewal and increased strength:

> *What joy for those whose strength comes from the LORD,*
> *who have set their minds on a pilgrimage to*
> *Jerusalem.*
> When they walk through the Valley of Weeping,
> it will become a place of refreshing springs.
> *The autumn rains will clothe it with blessings.*
> *They will continue to grow stronger,*
> *and each of them will appear before God in*
> *Jerusalem.*[4]

We must be a people "who have set their minds on a pilgrimage." We must keep our eyes on what God is doing next in our lives. He is always doing something new, though sometimes, He points out, we don't notice:

> *Forget the former things;*
> > *do not dwell on the past.*
> *See, I am doing a new thing!*
> > *Now it springs up; do you not perceive it?*[5]

Spring is coming soon. Our words must tell of it. Our mouths must sing of it. Our prayers must ask for it. Our actions must reflect it. Our lives must embrace it.

But sometimes looking toward tomorrow doesn't feel like looking toward spring. The Egyptian woman I met at the drugstore on Christmas Eve knows that her son will never have his hand back. We all have grieved loved ones we will never see again in this life. Some things will not go back to where they were before the storm blew in, but the intensity of the pain will pass, and you will walk in better weather. Even concerning death, we "do not grieve like the rest of mankind, who have no hope."[6] Some things may be lost forever during winter, but we never stop praying and living expectantly for the creative ways that God will restore, not only our situations, but *us*.

Heaven is a guarantee. Always look forward.

The Spirit of God whets our appetite by giving us a taste of what's ahead. He puts a little of heaven in our hearts so that we'll never settle for less.

That's why we live with such good cheer. You won't see us drooping our heads or dragging our feet! Cramped conditions here don't get us down. They only remind us of the spacious living conditions ahead. It's what we trust in but don't yet see that keeps us going. Do you suppose a few ruts in the road or rocks in the path are going to stop us? When the time comes, we'll be plenty ready to exchange exile for homecoming.[7]

• • •

Spring will be a season when new beauty grows in our lives in ways we cannot imagine right now. We can wait for it with glad wonder. We can wait for it with renewed joy.

We can wait for the day we will bloom.

But hoping for change in front of the watching world can be almost embarrassing. What if we never get what we hope for? What if it all was in vain? Isn't it true that "hope deferred makes the heart sick"?[8]

We don't have to worry about that. God knows what's at stake in our waiting. He puts Himself into the process, no matter how the process ends. Paul wrote that "hope does not put us to shame, because God's love has been poured out into our hearts through the Holy Spirit, who has been given to us."[9] We can base all of our confidence upon "Christ in [us], the hope of glory."[10] Hope is this: the Creator within His creation.

In a way, we are the seeds of Eden, ever becoming the glorious garden of the Master Gardener. Jesus came so that the people of God could be "oaks of righteousness, a planting of the Lord for the display of his splendor."[11] He knows that what begins by being buried in darkness eventually reaches for the sky.

The hope we are hunting has been within us all along. When seeds are broken, they release growth. And when God's people are broken, they release hope.

ACKNOWLEDGMENTS

I am indebted to Dr. Bill and Jan Howard, who shared their little cabin so that I could hear the Lord's whisper in the woods.

Thank you to the prayer and review team, who began praying when I had nothing but a notebook I had filled in a cabin: Becky Brooks, DeeAnn Brownlow, Dr. Larry and Joan Calvin, Candy Dodd, Pam Hawkins, Brian Huff, Christi Littlefield (the best freshman roommate ever), Emily Macht, Carol Maples, Mark and Tara Maples, Staci Markwood, Chantelle Read, Russ Pennington, Lisa Phillips, Brenda Riebkes, Debbie Rife, Michelle Stiles, and Maci Wilson. And to Dr. David Hampson and Dr. Jim Mann.

Thank you to the Around My Table girls, who prayed after the notebook became my manuscript: Pam Branscum, Mary Cobb, Trina Derr, Lisa Fraze, Dereca Gist, Randi Freeby, Shannon Herman, Suzy Jeffrey, Stephanie Northam, Amanda Orr, Jennifer Owen, Courtney Shuman, Cyndi Spraggins, Chesley Walton, and Shelly Ward.

Thank you to Frank Breeden, who agreed that my manuscript should become a book.

Thank you to Pamela Clements and everyone at Worthy Publishing, who made it so.

And thank You, God, for whispering in the first place.

NOTES

Introduction
1. Psalm 18:11
2. Exodus 20:21
3. 2 Corinthians 6:4–10 NLT
4. 2 Corinthians 6:2
5. 1 John 1:5
6. John 1:5 NLT
7. John 8:12 NLT
8. Isaiah 45:7 NKJV
9. Isaiah 61:3
10. Romans 8:31
11. Genesis 50:20
12. Philippians 3:10
13. 1 Peter 1:6–7
14. Joel 2:21

Chapter One
1. Matthew 29:39
2. Romans 5:2–5
3. 1 Peter 1:7 NLT
4. Psalm 89:8 NLT
5. John 9:3 NLT
6. John 11:4 NLT
7. 2 Corinthians 12:9

Chapter Two
1. Psalm 46:10 NLT
2. 2 Corinthians 1:3–7 NLT
3. Marco A. Torres, "Locked Away: A Tour of Harvard Yard's Neglected Gates," *Harvard Crimson*, October 3, 2013, http://www.thecrimson.com/article/2013/10/3/locked-away/?page=1.

Chapter Three
1. Numbers 14:21–23 NLT
2. Deuteronomy 1:2
3. Deuteronomy 1:39 NLT
4. Romans 12:2
5. 1 Corinthians 1:27 NLT
6. Isaiah 55:9
7. Daniel 10:12

Chapter Four
1. Luke 11:5–10 NLT
2. Luke 18:1–8 NLT
3. 1 Thessalonians 5:17 NASB
4. James 1:5–7 NLT

Chapter Five
1. Job 38:3
2. Job 38:22–30

Chapter Six
1. Hebrews 4:12
2. Isaiah 40:6–8 NLT
3. Ephesians 6:11, 17

Chapter Seven
1. James 4:8 NKJV
2. Psalm 139:1–5 NLT
3. Matthew 28:20 NLT
4. Lamentations 2:19 NKJV

Chapter Eight
1. Matthew 5:21–22
2. Matthew 5:27
3. Matthew 5:38
4. 2 Corinthians 5:10

NOTES

5. Matthew 7:3–5 NLT
6. Revelation 3:7 NLT

Chapter Nine
1. Revelation 1:5 NLT
2. Psalm 107:2 NLT
3. Revelation 12:11 NKJV

Chapter Ten
1. Proverbs 17:22

Chapter Eleven
1. Romans 3:3–4 NIV1984
2. 2 Timothy 2:13

Chapter Fourteen
1. Luke 1:30
2. Matthew 10:28
3. John 10:10
4. Galatians 5:25
5. Joshua 1:7–8 NLT
6. John 8:43–47 NLT

Chapter Fifteen
1. Proverbs 18:22 NLT
2. Exodus 3:13–15
3. Galatians 2:20 ESV

Chapter Sixteen
1. 2 Kings 21:16 NLT
2. 2 Chronicles 33:10 MSG
3. 2 Kings 21:13
4. 2 Chronicles 33:11–12 MSG
5. 2 Chronicles 33:12–13 MSG
6. Ephesians 2:10
7. 1 Peter 4:5–7 MSG
8. Proverbs 16:18

Chapter Seventeen
1. Matthew 5:39 MSG
2. Luke 7:39 MSG
3. Luke 7:47–48 NLT

Chapter Nineteen
1. 2 Corinthians 4:6–10 NLT
2. John 16:33
3. Numbers 32:6–7 NLT
4. Dallas Willard, *The Divine Conspiracy* (New York: HarperCollins, 1998), 399.

Chapter Twenty
1. A. J. Russell, ed., *God Calling* (New York: Jove Books, 1978), 71.
2. Revelation 12:11
3. Nehemiah 8:10 NLT
4. Psalm 84:5–7 NLT
5. Isaiah 43:18–19
6. 1 Thessalonians 4:13
7. 2 Corinthians 5:5–8 MSG
8. Proverbs 13:12
9. Romans 5:5
10. Colossians 1:27
11. Isaiah 61:3

ABOUT THE AUTHOR

Nika Maples is the author of *Twelve Clean Pages*, the memoir of her survival of lupus and a stroke that left her quadriplegic at age twenty. After learning to walk and talk again, she became a public school teacher, winning 2007 Texas Secondary Teacher of the Year. She holds an MA in English Education from Columbia University and currently is pursuing an MDiv from The King's University. When she is not traveling to speak, she lives, writes, and laughs as much as possible in Fort Worth, Texas.

WWW.NIKAMAPLES.COM

IF YOU ENJOYED THIS BOOK, WILL YOU CONSIDER SHARING THE MESSAGE WITH OTHERS?

Recommend it to those in your small group, book club, or class.

Connect with Nika at facebook.com/nikamaples and post a comment or photo.

Share an image of hope in your world on Instagram and join the #huntinghope photo stream.

Tweet "I am a hope hunter. @nikamaples // @worthypub"

Pick up a copy for someone who would be challenged and encouraged by this message.